HEBREW
ISRAELITES
Identity Revealed

A Narrative of the Black Hebrew
Israelites and the Bantus of the World

THOMAS T. GAKURU

Tony Nganga Press
A Division of
Amazon Publishing Platform
Email: tonyngangapress@gmail.com

"Speaking to the Purposes of God for this
Generation and for the Generations to Come"

ISBN-13: 978-1722968113
ISBN-10: 1722968117

Unless otherwise identified,
Scriptures marked KJV are taken from the KING JAMES VERSION (KJV): KING JAMES VERSION, public domain.
Brief quotations taken from Zondervan Bible Dictionary with permission.

Printed in the United States of America
Printed in Kenya with permission from the publisher by;

Tafsiri Printing Press
Tafsiriprintingpress@btlkenya.co.ke

Preface

This book is the epic saga of the Children of God. The writer traces the children of Israel from the patriarch Noah, through a journey of approximately 4365 years. It is their relationship between their God, brethren and neighbors that is unearthed. It's a journey wrought with many challenges from within and without the family of Israel. Sometimes the reader is challenged to put into perspective the promises of God and the actions of His Children, culminating in the outcome. In hindsight it does not seem plausible for a people so blessed by having the Mighty and living God as their benefactor, to disregard their good fortune to pursue short term pleasures of being in sync with their pagan neighbors. But we all see these traits in ourselves and others all the time, and we call it peer influence.

We therefore should not condemn them of their apparent foolishness but look inward and learn. God is the Almighty God; He is no respecter of persons; His word is His bond; one thousand years to Him is like a day. When you view this chessboard of God and His relationship with His Children, do not be conceited, but be in awe and fear Him. Do your soul searching for in His infinite mercy all are accommodated. Rejecting Him will have catastrophic and permanent repercussions, while accepting Him will usher eternal bliss in His presence. Like David said in, Psalms 84:10; *"For a day in Your courts is better than a thousand. I would rather be a doorkeeper in the house of my God than to dwell in the tents of wickedness."*

Read this book and read again, do your own due diligence and counter referencing. Keep your bible handy for it's your sure authority. It's the life story of YHWH and His children. What is presented here is just but a small part, a start and hopefully a push to realign your life to mirror your God through His son Jesus Christ. This book is intended to be small, easy to read and memorable in order to egg you on in this adventure of discovery about this life. It's not for the faint hearted, for those willing to travel this road must open their mind to new possibilities. What they have always held as true will be challenged. The ultimate goal of enlightenment and decision making is a personal journey and responsibility.

THOMAS T. GAKURU

Dedication

I dedicate this book to my grandchildren, without who our lineage would wither. I bless you all, be fruitful and multiply, may you be prosperous and excel in your fields. May you be leaders in your generations, to lead our people in paths of righteousness.

AMEN.

Acknowledgement

I want to acknowledge the inspirational, revelation and insightful thoughts, ideas and the grace that our God, the Almighty YHWH, the LORD GOD of our fathers, Abraham, Isaac and Jacob has bestowed upon me, His child. Without Him in my life this knowledge about our identity as the chosen children of God would never have happened. I give Him all praises and honor.

My heartfelt thanks go to my wife Esther, who prompted and encouraged me in this journey. As my confidant, she alone shared the pain I felt for our ancestors, she also shared the joys and excitement of discovery about our heritage. She sacrificed our time together for this work to be accomplished. I sincerely thank you.

My special thanks go to our sons Derrick and Julian also their wives Gina and Phiona respectfully. They encouraged, gave tips and infused enthusiasm that is only possible with the youth. May our God bless them with the abundance of His grace.

I acknowledge my publisher Pastor Tony Nganga, who God connected us, when I was at a cross road. He provided solutions far beyond my expectations. May God bless you!

CONTENTS

Chapter 1

INTRODUCTION

This Chapter is meant to establish the unity of the Kikuyu people in bringing up their children, and how information was disseminated to the younger generations through story telling. This way morals and uprightness were highly held. Every age-group was taught the cultural practices of the people at different stages of life, commensurate to their duties. The stories were enhanced with the right proverbs, sayings and metaphors.

Folk Lore

Along time ago in a village far away there was a very beautiful girl named Muthaka. Now Muthaka was not your ordinary kind of girl. Not only was she the most beautiful of all, she was also the daughter of a very wealthy chief. He had many herds of cattle, goats and sheep. He had servants and many fertile farms. Muthaka was also a gifted girl in many areas. Being the chief's daughter, she learned early the art of entertainment and she had a good heart. All the young men in the village desired to marry her, but to their dismay none proved worthy of her hand in marriage. She never refused to entertain any of them, but they all failed her tests. Young men from other ridges came to try their luck but failed. Her father, the chief had promised to support her choice.

One day two young men came from a far country to try their luck. One was very handsome, tall and masculine. Everybody was sure he was the one. His name was Kahenia. His mate Keega was the opposite in everything and nobody gave him a second glance.

Muthaka entertained the young men and offered each a heavily laden half-calabash of the best sweet potatoes you ever tasted. As they ate she busied herself elsewhere. Kahenia to enhance his chances secretly placed most of the peels of the sweet potatoes he had eaten on Keega's side. This would prove to the girl that keega was a glutton because his pile would be bigger. Of this Keega was aware, but since he had a good heart and did not want to compete with his friend, he let it slide. When they were finished eating Muthaka came to enquire of their business.

When they explained, Muthaka looked at the small pile of peels on Kahenia's side and then looked at Keega's pile. Unbeknown to them, she was able to discern what had transpired. She addressed the suitors and said "In all my life I've never seen a man with a bigger appetite than Keega, this means he will be a good provider. In view of this I accept his hand in marriage."

Moral of the story

Be your best self, it's the heart that matters.

It was a dark night and the hyenas were howling something awful. There didn't seem to be any escape from our impending doom. Have you ever seen a hyena's bite? It's got one of the strongest jaws of any animal. To make matters worse they hunt in packs. Five or even twenty of them. And this was a large pack. They demolish a grown cow in no time, skin, hooves and all. They are even known to crush the knee bone.

Now it seems our time had come, we could even see their eyes darting in the bushes nearby. We were in a circle crouching together back to back. Our spears, clubs and swords drawn and ready for the impending attack. With our hearts pounding, sweaty hands and dry mouth we knew it wouldn't be long. We had been shouting ourselves hoarse to try to scare them away, to no avail. Our leader, the immovable Njamba sounded strong, he was our pillar of strength, but this time hope was elusive. They came nearer and nearer. We could smell their foul breaths. Then just as they were about to pounce one squeaked and they vanished into the bushes like magic.

We hadn't heard it, but it was there!

Okay everybody time to sleep!

The rest of the story tomorrow.

Nobody argued with Njoroge about his stories. Who could sleep now with all this adrenaline pumping. But off we went theorizing what had saved these warriors.

This was how information was passed on from generation to generation about historical events, wars, famines and just plain old fables told and re-told around the fire place. This was while waiting for dinner to be ready, while eating and before bedtime. These stories would bring the families together. The adults all-knowing grins and the children wide eyed with fright or expectations. Sometimes you could hear squeaks, ahaa's or just laughter.

Those were the good old days and a lot of information was delivered to the next generation in this manner around a fire place. Stories would be told and retold repeatedly from generation to generation until all knew. Usually the best story teller would command the largest crowds.

This was Central Kenya in Africa. Then the white man happened. Everything changed. This was not your ordinary kind of enemy. Our people were not unfamiliar with warfare as a matter of fact we were good and held up to even the fiercest of them all. The Maasai! We would raid them, and they would raid us. The common merchandise was cattle, girls and children. Cattle made the raiders wealthier, girls to marry and children to weaken the victim and strengthen the raiders. All this was to make the tribe more prosperous and secure.

But the white man was something else. He came wielding a bible and gun. They subjugated and stayed. They made those they conquered virtual slaves. They settled themselves in our fertile lands and made us work for them. Deep inside we knew this was not the first or second time this was happening. White people had done this to us before, for it was whispered. And this is the story I want to whisper to you. What I'm just about to whisper to you has been whispered for generations. It is your heritage.

The ancestry of the Agikuyu (the Kikuyu of Kenya).

The ancestry of the BANTUS worldwide.

This whisper is for the BANTUS of the world. Those of the Gikuyu tribe of Kenya, all those of Africa and the world. All of them can relate to this saga, for it's their story. They may now be called Asians, Indians, Chinese, Mexicans, African Americans; Ibos of Nigeria; Sukuma of Tanzania; Xhosa, Lemba or Zulu of South Africa and many more all over the world but they all remain BANTUS. In some places, they are called by other names like Negros, Africans, Afros, etcetera. Some are hidden among Caucasians, Asians and Africans, knowingly or not. Others who are not Bantus, like the Europeans and Africans, can gain important information about themselves and their relationship to others. It's an eye opener to all who profess to know God. It also shows how they have been lied to.

We no longer have story telling around the fire place anymore, so this whisper I must pen for you.

The origin of the Kikuyu people of Kenya; more appropriately the GIKUYU people. They are said to have emerged at a place known as 'Mukurwe-in-wa-Nyagathanga'.

Chapter 2

BANTU MIGRATION IN AFRICA

In this chapter, we will look into one of the possible scenarios that settled a people of unknown origin, in the heart of Africa, from around 1500 B.C.E. This hypothetical conjecture is not intended to be viewed as fact, but as a possible explanation of events before the myth of Kikuyu supposed origin at Mukurwe-ini-wa-Nyagathanga. And there are many.

The Trek – The Gikuyu People of Kenya

It started a long time ago, in a far land to the North of present day Kenya. A band of travelers were hastily travelling South by South-East led by an astute man of about 50 years old. He had a mean hard look, just short of being handsome. He seemed to know their route, and the whole group had trust in him.

The group, comprising about 70 men, with women and children was among others travelling South and East, and other's Westwards. They were in a hurry, but cautious. Look-outs and scouts were maintained to all flanks. It was obvious this group was not a war party, and they were avoiding contact with local communities, who were scattered far and wide. They made their passage as inconspicuous as possible. Following them was made harder by their travelling as much as possible at night. If it rained, they stayed put, to leave no tracks. Their route was crafted much earlier by scouting the best route for concealment and rest areas.

This group was running away from something. Where they originated, they were not speaking much of. The younger ones were not aware of where they came from or where they were headed. Travelling seemed like all they did. Caution was instilled in all of them. There had been rumors of similar bands escaping. Some made it and others got caught or were allegedly killed by their pursuers. Those caught and killed were the lucky ones for slavery was worse. But the lure of freedom was overpowering. Stories of lands further to the south and west where our people could settle circulated.

The rumors of a savior were also rife. The people believed that one day a king would come and liberate them and punish their enemies. Those that decided to escape believed that when their savior conquered their enemies they would all know, so they could go back home. Days and nights passed without major problems, but one

day their luck ran out. The atmosphere changed, everybody became more alert, the normal banter of camp life changed. Movement and talk even within the camp was subdued. There was talk of a war party pursuing. Their worst nightmare was happening. Preparations for defense were apparent. Those able to fight were readied for the forthcoming confrontation. As the time became eminent one family made a pain-full decision. The head of the family called his twenty-year-old son and conveyed his instructions.

The young man was not completely learned in their ways but what he knew would have to suffice. He knew they were running away to freedom, to a place they knew nothing about. He knew it would be better than slavery or death. He also knew the danger the journey entailed. His father and the community had trained him in many things pertaining to survival and adulthood. Although his training was not complete, he was well trained.

"Son, he told him, it is now eminent that we are going to fight, and our survival is very slim. For us as a people we must somehow survive if only some of us. Our people have known sacrifices before and this is your time. What I'm about to ask you to do is your contribution to our community. I've dreaded this time might come, and I trained you for this very purpose, to survive. You are young, but your outlook and decision making are beyond your years. You can survive anywhere, you can wrestle a living where others would give up. I wish I had more time to be with you, we love you, but I've decided to let you go on your own. The little time we have before you go will be for your final preparations.

When the time comes, I want you to sneak out of camp and swiftly get away following the instructions I will give you. I know you are a good long-distance runner, and few can keep up with you. Navigate with the sun and stars like I taught you. You are strong and intelligent, and the fighting skills I taught you have been passed on from our people for ages. Keep practicing and as you mature you will become better. I'm separating you, because alone you have the best chance of survival. We might never meet again but if it's the LORD'S will we shall.

I would have liked to send you with your sister, but this would only slow you down. This would endanger you and we cannot risk that. Cruel as it might look, your survival is the survival of our lineage. Her survival would only benefit another people where she gets married, because you cannot

marry her. Our lineage flows from father to son only.

Again, I reiterate, after you get to destination go on with your life waiting for our unification but knowing it might never happen. With this the father blessed his son with the blessing of his ancestors and their God. All that they waited for was the opportunity to depart."

And depart he did. Several nights later the attack happened. About half the travelers were killed. In the confusion, nobody knew where the young man went. Some were dispersed, others killed while others survived and continued. Unbeknown to most, the young man did not go alone. He had confided his plan to a young girl who was the love of his life. They managed to escape together in the melee. She was a spirited beautiful girl. She was tough and able to endure hardships. When she whispered their plan to her parents they released her without fuss.

The survivors managed to press on with their journey, much depleted in strength, but even more determined. The two parties like the young man's father predicted, never met again. It is whispered that many bands like these made these dangerous trips to escape persecution. Wherever they went, they were hardy enough to persevere and sometimes dominate the communities they encountered and sometimes assimilate them altogether. They penetrated Africa mainly to the west. Others went south. These forced migrations happened at varied times in history. Some never met their own people again. Others left together and after a separation would meet again after a long time like fifty years. These people had migrated before and some could remember stories where their ancestors had made similar journeys. They knew one day they would go back home. They also knew, if they were destined to go back home they must reproduce or become extinct. Wherever they went, they became productive and multiplied.

The young couple after their hasty departure, managed to elude any would be enemies completely. They travelled in sections all the time hoping against hope their families would catch up. They would set camp on high ground and visually scout large tracts of land in the hope of seeing any sign. After staying a while they would move on. They left very little sign of their passage to elude their enemies. Their encounter with locals was very limited, far and wide. They progressively went south overcoming many hazards like heat, cold, rain and wild animals until they sighted their destination, the snowcapped mountain at the equator. This became their beacon and they bore right as if to go around it. The mountain was several thousand feet high with varied vegetation, most of which was thick forests. The climate around the mountain was very varied, from warm to very cold. The higher you went the colder it became, especially at night.

After scouting the land, they settled at a place to the South of the mountain. They built a shelter which was circular, the walls were made of poles stuck into the ground; interwoven with sapling and filled in with mud reinforced with grass. The roof was grass thatch. It was one room, with one area designated as kitchen and another as sleeping quarters. It also doubled as granary and store. This place had good rivers, animals to hunt and arable land. All these considerations were imperative to their survival. After some time, they discovered a village a few miles to their west. They knew they had to move on but delayed their departure because of the investment they had made improving their homestead. Another consideration was they needed to learn the ways and language of these people. They would hide in the bushes and listen in, and in a short while they could understand the language and culture. They helped each other practice speaking it. They learned a lot and it became an adventure. They were sure they could stay hidden for a long time. Also, they knew if their families ever came they would need to interact with their neighbors.

Then one day the inevitable happened. By now our young couple were about twenty-three years old, tough as nails. They had proved their survival skills. They could wrestle a living anywhere, and this may have made them less cautious. One-day, late afternoon, as they were stalking game they encountered young warriors from the nearby village. There was no escape. After sizing them up the warriors started snickering and talking about what they would do to the young couple especially the young woman. To them it was obvious they were foreigners. They even started negotiating who would make her his wife. All this time they had no inkling the young couple could understand what was being said. The toughest looking warrior was sizing the young man, and confidently declared, whoever kills the young man would have the girl.

All this time the young couple feigned ignorance of the evil designs of the warriors. They conferred in their language and made plans of how to counter the attack. When it came, they were ready. The young man carried with him bows and arrows which were useless in this confrontation. He also carried a stick. It was about six feet and about one-and-a-half-inch diameter. The stick, hard as iron came from a hard wood from up north, treated with salts and oil. It did not look threatening or dangerous but, in the hands of a trained stick fighter it was lethal. It was the perfect weapon for close quarter fighting. It could be used for killing if necessary.

The seven warriors were confident because of their numerical advantage. They carried with them spears, clubs, bows and arrows. To any observer this was no contest, the young man would be overwhelmed, killed and his girl taken. Case closed, or so it seemed. Then the contest started becoming interesting. As the warriors got near the stick would dart out and strike. The movement was so quick they never saw it coming. Within a short while the young man managed to push and herd the warriors to one side. His girl was behind him and he positioned himself in such a way that they could only attack him from one side. The girl was also not helpless, any warrior who came near was hit and repelled using the quiver she held for the young man. The warriors got into each other's way and made a mess of everything. They got a thrashing of their life. Their joints and major muscle groups got the blunt of the young man's punishing blows. There was no blood or cracked bones, but the cries and yelps told a story of anguish like they had never experienced. When all the attackers were laid down in total surrender, the punishment stopped. The young couple departed. In the whole encounter, they never let out they could understand the local language.

Several days later an old man and two boys visited the young couple. Of course, the young couple knew this was the chief of the village where the attackers came from. One of the boys carried a stool for the chief to sit on; the other carried a shoulder bag with stuff for the chief. The chief wore a two-piece attire, with animal skin loin skirt held together with a leather strap. The skirt came around the knees. A shoulder shawl was draped over his shoulders covering his upper torso and at the front held together with leather straps. On his feet, he wore leather sandals. On his hand, he wielded a thin reed. His head was adorned with a feather decorated head gear. You could see he was an important man. Like his compatriots, his skin was a dark color with block shaped head, unlike the young couple, whose color was lighter and oval shaped head, otherwise they looked similar. The boys wore only a simple skirt and were otherwise un-adorned.

When the chief reached the center of the compound belonging to the young couple he hailed to announce himself. The young couple came out of their shelter where they had been watching from. When the chief greeted them with much gesturing, for he thought they did not understand his language, they simply replied the greetings using the proper address for the chief. The chief was dumfounded, but he recovered quickly. After pleasantries were dispensed with, the chief enquired of the young couple where they came from, and their intentions. He learned they were the advanced party and their people would be coming soon. To this information, the chief made a quick decision. If this one youngster could beat his warriors thus, then what would happen when the main party arrived?

He bid the young couple welcome, for much of the land was uninhabited. They agreed to meet the next day on a high ground up the slopes of the mountain (Kiri-Nyaga). This was so they could agree on boundaries between their two communities.

On the appointed day, they met on the agreed location.

From their vantage point they could see the big mountain to the south (Kilimanjaro) and the ranges (aberdares) to the west. The chief pointed to the south west a clearing with a big tree. He described the location where the young man could locate his homestead. They also agreed on their common boundary using features on the ground like rivers and hills. They agreed to be good neighbors and assist one another when in need. After this agreement, they all went to the chief's village, where they had a celebration. The young couple received lots of gifts. Unfortunately, the warriors they had encountered with were still in 'intensive care' being massaged with castor oil. They could not enjoy the celebrations.

After leaving their new-found neighbors, the young couple journeyed South to the agreed spot. The journey was through rough and forested terrain rife with many wild animals. The rivers flowing from the mountain and ranges had cut deep valleys which were treacherous to cross. After some days, through thick forest, they EMERGED at *"mukurwe-ini-wa-nyagathanga"* the grove they had agreed with the chief. This is in present day Muranga County.

They set up their home-stead near a big fig tree (Gikuyu). A normal fig tree is called a "mukuyu". Prefix "Gi-' denotes big in size. The young couple settled and thrived. The neighbors referred to the place as 'Gwa-Gikuyu' (Gikuyu's place) because of the big fig tree in his compound and his rangy stature, and the name stuck. He became the father of the Gikuyu tribe. The young woman whose vocation was pottery was referred to as Mumbi (creator) because of her beautiful creations. Although they never re-united with their families, they later integrated with other escapees who settled nearby. Some of these escapees had migrated earlier through the west African route. Others directly south like the young couple. Some of these are known as the Kamba's, Meru's, Chaggas, Embu's etcetera.

The couple became famous because of their exploits, and people sought their friendship. They were hard working and generous. As they grew older they were blessed with nine daughters plus one. When the nine daughters were ready for marriage Gikuyu was in a dilemma because there were no suitable young men to marry them. One day he went up the *Kiri-Nyaga* Mountain and prayed to God for a solution to his problem. It is whispered that God heard his prayers and miraculously nine young men appeared and married his daughters. The nine clans of the Agikuyu (people of Gikuyu) people are named after these daughters of Gikuyu. Every kikuyu can identify with one of these clans. Some of the girl's names and clans are; Wambui – Ambui, Wacera – Acera, Wanjiru-Anjiru and so on.

That was one saga of the Bantu people that produced a tribe in the heart of Africa. Now the Agikuyu's number more than ten million. They are the largest tribe in modern day Kenya and they occupy the slopes of Mt. Kenya (Kiri-Nyaga) and other places in Kenya and around the world.

Egypt, West Africa, Congo/Niger and Beyond

Other trekkers took different routes, but the main route was to West Africa. From West Africa, some stayed, while others moved to Central Africa in the Congo-Niger region. Some settled in Congo-Niger region while others moved on to East Africa and others went all the way South to South Africa, leaving some enroute. All these different routes made it difficult to rejoin a group if separated. Others reunited after a long time. As years passed after these migrations, language and culture changed. Other factors that brought this difference was interaction with local communities and colonial subjugation. But one thing remained consistent, their Bantu identity. Most of these communities still retain over 80% of their Bantu identity.

The periods of these migrations, routes and reasons are very varied and separated by centuries. Despite this, some traits come through, like worship practices, architecture, cultural rites like marriage, coming of age and age group. Now they are all colors, creed and sizes. Recently, I heard of Chinese Bantus. There are concentrations of the Bantu people in Africa, the Americas and Islands, Asia, Europe and Australia. They are referred to by all kinds of names like Agikuyu, Akamba, Miji-kenda, Ibos, Chaggas, Indians, Africans, African or Afro-Americans, Luhyas, Baganda's, Kisii's, Negroes, Natives and many more.

The whisper of the Bantu migration is one of forced migration, to escape persecution and slavery. It is even whispered that the Agikuyu of Kiambu escaped Muranga because of bad medicine. The easy demeanor of the Bantus has caused others to subjugate them, like the British colonialists, the Belgian King Leopold and his rubber plantations, the Italians, Arabs, Africans, Germans and Spaniards, all had a hand in colonizing or enslaving the Bantu. In General, the Europeans, Africans and Arabs have been the main culprits.

Even after these forced migrations some were captured, killed, tortured and sold as slaves in the Americas, Europe and the Arab world. Some are still enslaved in North Africa and the Middle East. A lot of trauma has been visited on the Bantu. Literally, all the races of the world have ganged up to oppress the Bantu. They have used the Bantu's resources of labor and raw materials to build and enrich their economies. All the economies of the ancient and modern world were built on the back of the Bantu.

It is said that if a community is conquered frequently, their stock of knowledge can be reduced to primitivity. This happens because the conquerors will kill or carry away the productive ones leaving the weak, old and very young. By the time the young are old enough to receive from the older folks, they are harvested again, and the older folks fade away thereby disrupting generational hand over. Because of these upheavals, the Bantus have lost a lot, primarily in the way of identity to an extent most don't know where they originated from or who they are.

Why is this so? Maybe by the end of this whisper we will put the pieces together and establish the reason for this mal-treatment. To do this, we must find out where these Bantus came from, why they are everybody's punching bag. And the place to start? The beginning of-course! And the beginning is after the deluge; and the survivors of the flood. Noah's flood. In the bible.

*In this chapter it is easy to see our fore fathers hid something from us. They also left a clue to tell us so! It is common knowledge that family lineage is from father to son in most cultures, more so the Bantus. If this is true, how come the children of Gikuyu did not inherit their lineage from the men who married Gikuyu's daughters? Also, the Agikuyu refer themselves as "Nyumba ya Mumbi" (House of Mumbi). This raises another question, did Gikuyu have other wives or were there other houses other than Mumbi's in Gikuyu's family? Or, did Gikuyu perform another Lot affair with his daughters to preserve their heritage? And if the story is true, how come all clans share the same genetic information? The answer to me seems to be, **Gikuyu had sons not daughters**!*

Another omission – how come our history suddenly starts at Mukurwe-ini-wa Nyagathanga –what about before that?

Chapter 3

SONS OF NOAH

It is established that many communities that kept their history for a long time, had a deluge story. We find one in the bible. In this story of Genesis, God wiped out almost all of humankind. He started again what He had done at creation, only this time there were eight people. These eight especially the Sons of Noah became our ancestors. It is here we will start our search of where the Bantus came from.

The Three and their Regional Descendants

We have all heard or read the bible story of Noah's flood. It's actually not Noah's flood because he never caused it. He only survived because, unlike his compatriots, he believed when God whispered to him about the coming flood that would cleanse the earth of all evil that was widespread. He prophesied to his neighbors who did not believe him.

Why are we dwelling on this Noah flood? The reason is simple. After the flood, only eight people survived. These were Noah, his wife, his three sons and each his wife.

We read In Gen 9:18-19; "And the sons of Noah, that went forth of the ark, were Shem, and Ham, and Japheth: and Ham is the father of Canaan.

These are the three sons of Noah: and of them was the whole earth overspread."

Let's look at the lineage of the three. The bible in Gen 10 and 11 charts out each of the three families;

JAPHETH begat

Gomar, Magog, Madai, Javan, Tubal, Meshech and Tiras.

Gomar begat **Ashkenaz**, Riphath and Torgarmar.

Javan begat – Elishah, Tarshish, Kittim and Dodanim.

These inhabited Asia Minor, the Caucuses, Western and Eastern Europe. They are known as the Asians and Europeans.

HAM bega0074

Cush (Ethiopians), Mizraim (Egyptians), Put (Libyans), Canaan.

Cush begat Seba, Havilah, Sabtah, Raamah, Sabtechah and Nimrod.

Mizraim begat Ludim, Anamim, Lehabim, Naphtuhim, Pathrusim, and Casluhim

Canaan begat Sidon, Heth, Jebusite, Amorite, Girgashite, Hivite, Arkite, Sinite, Arvadite, Zemarite and Hamthite.

These are Africans and they settled in Africa except Canaan who settled in Mesopotamia.

SHEM begat

Elam, Asshur, Arphaxad, Lud, Aram

Aram begat Uz, Hul, Gether, Mash

Arphaxad begat Salah, Eber

Eber begat Peleg and Joktan

Joktan begat Almodad, Sheleph, Hazarmareth, Jerah, Hadoram, Uzal, Diklah, Obal, Abimaeh, Sheba, Ophir, Havilah, Jobab

Peleg begat Reu, Serug, Nahor, Terah,

Terah begat Abram, Nahor, Haran

Haran begat Lot

Abram begat Ishmael, Isaac

Ishmael the father of the twelve Ishmaelite princes

Isaac begat Esau, Jacob

Esau the father of the **Edomite**'s

Jacob the father of the Twelve Tribes of **Israel**

These are the Semites and they settled in Mesopotamia.

Japheth is the ancestor of the people living in Europe and Asia. They are the Europeans and Asians. The most visible players of the house of Japheth in bible history, are the Romans. In their adventures they intermingled with the Edomites to such an extent the Edomites, who are Hebrew children of Esau disappeared. They became one. The Romans also intermingled with Europeans of the house of Japheth. They are now widespread in the whole of the European world.

The children of Ham are in North Africa. Mizraim is the Egyptians; Put is the Libyans; Cush is the Ethiopians; and Canaan settled in Mesopotamia. Why Canaan settled in Mesopotamia is of interest. This will answer the question why God promised the Hebrews land occupied by others.

According to the book of Jubilees chapter 10:27-32;

"In the fourth week in the first year in the beginning thereof in the four and thirtieth jubilee, were they dispersed from the land of Shinar. (*This is referring to the dispersal of people at the tower of Babel. When the people of earth led by Nimrod son of Cush decided to build a tower to heaven, God confused their language and they could not communicate in one language like before. That is how we got many languages.*)

And Ham and his sons went into the land which he was to occupy, which he acquired as his portion in the land of the south.

And Canaan saw the land of Lebanon to the river of Egypt that it was very good, and he went not into the land of his inheritance to the west that is to the sea, and he dwelt there in the land of Lebanon, eastward and westward from the border of Jordan and from the border of the sea.

And Ham, his father and Cush and Mizraim, his brothers, said unto him: "thou hast settled in a land which is not thine, and that which did not fall to us by lot: do not do so; for if thou dost so, thou and thy sons will fall in the land and be accursed through sedition; for by sedition ye have settled, and by sedition will thy children fall, and thou shall be rooted out for ever. Dwell not in the dwelling of Shem; for to Shem and to his sons did it come by their lot.

Cursed art thou, and cursed shall thou be beyond all the sons of Noah, by the curse by which we bound ourselves by an oath in the presence of the holy judge, and in the presence of Noah our father.

But he did not hearken unto them, and dwelt in the land of Lebanon from Hamarth to the entering of Egypt, he and his sons until this day".

Note: *(during the exodus, God told the Children of Israel to go occupy the land of Canaan, to rout out the inhabitants. This did not look right until you knew that the Canaanites were occupying this land by sedition, for it really belonged to the Children of Shem)*

The Hamites are a black people found predominantly in Africa and the Middle East.

The house of Shem settled in Mesopotamia. As the lineage came nearer to the actors of today, we see in the lineage of Shem; Abram, Ishmael, Esau and Jacob coming to prominence.

Abraham (Abram) the father of Ismael and Isaac.

Ishmael was the father of the twelve princes.

Isaac had two sons Esau and Jacob.

Esau was the father of the Edomite's.

Jacob was the father of the twelve tribes of Israel.

God established an everlasting covenant with Abram to be God to him and his descendants after him. Abrams name was changed to Abraham and Sarai his wife was to be called Sarah. The outward sign was circumcision of all the male of his household. The land of Canaan was included as an everlasting possession. Meaning forever.

Ishmael was Abrams son with Hagar, the Egyptian handmaid to Sarai his wife. Sarai was barren. When God promised Abram a son she decided to 'help God' by giving Abram her handmaid Hagar, so that they could get a son through her. When the maid conceived, she despised her mistress, who complained to Abram. Abram told her that her maid was in her hand, thereby giving her license to deal with her harshly. This made Hagar to flee but was advised by the Angel of the LORD to return and promised a multitude of descendants.

Isaac was the son of promise that was covenanted between God and Abraham.

Isaac took Rebekah as wife.

We read In, Gen 25:21-34;

"And Isaac intreated the Lord for his wife, because she was barren: and the Lord was intreated of him, and Rebekah his wife conceived.

And the children struggled together within her; and she said, if it be so, why am I thus? And she went to enquire of the Lord.

And the Lord said unto her, two nations are in thy

womb, and two manner of people shall be separated from thy bowels; and the one people shall be stronger than the other people; and the elder shall serve the younger.

(This divine word-that the elder would serve the younger-explained the struggle within her, and later the reversal of inheritance custom whereby the elder would expect to be the heir and served by the younger)

And when her days to be delivered were fulfilled, behold, there were twins in her womb.

And the first came out red, all over like an hairy garment; and they called his name Esau.

And after that came his brother out, and his hand took hold on Esau's heel; and his name was called Jacob: and Isaac was threescore years old when she bare them.

And the boys grew: and Esau was a cunning hunter, a man of the field; and Jacob was a plain man, dwelling in tents.

And Isaac loved Esau, because he did eat of his venison: but Rebekah loved Jacob.

And Jacob sod pottage: and Esau came from the field, and he was faint:

And Esau said to Jacob, Feed me, I pray thee, with that

same red pottage; for I am faint: therefore was his name called Edom.

And Jacob said, Sell me this day thy birthright.

And Esau said, Behold, I am at the point to die: and what profit shall this birthright do to me?

And Jacob said, Swear to me this day; and he swore unto him: and he sold his birthright unto Jacob.

Then Jacob gave Esau bread and pottage of lentiles; and he did eat and drink, and rose up, and went his way: thus Esau despised his birthright."

As Isaac, neared death, he instructed his son Esau to prepare him a meal, in preparation to bless him. Rebekah overheard this and made plans to deceive her husband Isaac. Isaac ended up blessing Jacob which made him flee from his brother Esau and stay with his uncle for twenty years.

Jacob ended up being the carrier of Abrahams blessing. His name was changed to Israel and he became the father of the twelve tribes of Israel. Esau became the father of the Edomites.

In this introductory story of the origin of the people of the world as we know it, we see the children of Japheth being the Europeans and Asians. The children of Ham being the Africans, including the Canaanites who settled in Mesopotamia. The children of Shem that are of prominence are the Ishmaelites, the Israelites and the Edomites who are the children of Esau. They settled in Mesopotamia.

Chapter 4

BANTUS AND THE SONS OF NOAH

We will try to collate the information we have for the Bantus to find the closest relationship with the sons of Noah. We will start by striking out the least obvious and deal with the most likely.

Lineage - Elimination and Conjecture.

The Bantus as a people are of black complexion, found mainly in Africa South of the Sahara. They are also found in various concentrations all over the world. Their ancestry is not clear as their history is described from a migratory state not origin.

We have not established the genealogy of the Bantus prior to their migratory tendencies first reported in west Africa around 1500 B.C.E. There is no direct ancestral lineage from the sons of Noah to the Bantus. What we have established is that all people of earth are descended from the three sons of Noah. We have also established that the three settled with their families as follows;

Japheth settled North of Mesopotamia, this is

Europe and Asia. These people are white or red and various shades thereof; they are also called Caucasians in reference to their settling around the Caucasus Mountains. The Bantus are generally black, that's why the Spaniard explorers called them Negroes, meaning black. We can rule out Japheth being their ancestor.

Shem settled in Mesopotamia initially around the area of Shinar. The most visible children of Shem today are Ishmaelites, Edomites and Israelites. The Ishmaelites are still around in Mesopotamia and are generally referred to as Arabs. They do not share obvious characteristics with the Bantus and we rule them out as possible ancestors of the Bantus. The Edomites, being the children of Esau were generally not black but several shades red and they are thought to have integrated themselves with the Romans, and they became one.

The Israelites have a history of migratory tendencies. Some willingly and some forcibly taken mostly to or through Egypt, Europe (Rome) and Asia. These migrations are from the time of Joseph around 1700 B.C.E. to the Roman conquest of 70 and 135 C.E. when they were defeated with more than five hundred thousand killed, many sold into slavery and banished from Jerusalem. They disappeared into Africa, Asia and Europe. The color of their skin was not overly mentioned. From that time, they were in diaspora until 1948 when the State of Israel was established.

Ham settled mainly in Northern and North-Eastern of Africa. Their Identity is not in question as their history is well documented. They can trace their ancestry to Ham, the youngest son of Noah. According to the Zondervan Compact Bible Dictionary; "Ham - The youngest son of Noah, born probably about 96 years before the flood; and one of the eight persons to live through the flood. He became the progenitor of the dark races; **not the Negroes**, but the Egyptians, Ethiopians, Libyans and Canaanites." The Bantus have just been ejected from the African band-wagon! It is easy, but erroneous, to think the Bantus are Hamites, because they are overwhelmingly found in Africa and they are black.

But in view of the above we can state that the Bantus are not Hamites. The Canaanites settled in Mesopotamia in the land meant for the children of Shem.

The only people with close ties to the Bantus seem to be in the house of Shem - The Israelites!

There is a mystery in the saga of Israelite dispersal or migration starting as far back as 1700 B.C.E. to the final dispersal of around 135 C.E. Most of the time when they migrated they would go to Egypt. It is also with interest we note the sudden appearance of the Bantus within the same period of 1500 B.C.E. around the interior of Africa. One community with a well written history all the way to Noah and creation, gradually disappears while another, with no history of ancestry to Noah appears.

COULD THEY?

NOOOO!!

MAYBE.

These two communities need their histories investigated further to ascertain their relationship or lack thereof. With this in mind, we go back to the sons of Noah. Since none has a direct link to the Bantus we will use elimination to fish out the best possible lineage then seek possibilities and similarities.

One thing we do know, according to history and anthropology, the Bantus migrated from Northeast of Africa. This is the region of modern day Egypt. This area forms a land bridge connecting Europe, Africa and Asia. It is also a confluence of travel and trade routes between the three continents. This is also near the cradle of creation in Mesopotamia (Iraq) also known as the center of the earth. The Noah's Ark also rested nearby at Mt. Ararat. It seems obvious that when the Ark rested, the passengers would not go far to settle. When it came to divide the land among themselves; they went three ways from Mesopotamia. Japheth went North and East to Europe and Asia. Ham went South to Africa. Shem stayed put in Mesopotamia

What we do know is the Bantus migrated from around Egypt in Northeast Africa towards the West to West Africa, and some went South towards Ethiopia. From West Africa, they doubled back towards Central Africa. From Central Africa in the Congo Niger basin, some went East-ward to the Indian ocean coast while others South all the way to South Africa. All along the way some were left behind and formed communities. What were they running away from or what were they pursuing? Whatever it was they ended up in Africa. The northern part of Africa was occupied by the sons of Ham. These are the Egyptians, Ethiopians and Libyans. Canaanites settled in Mesopotamia.

From Africa, the Bantus dispersed further to the Americas, Asia, the Arab World, Europe and Australia.

The period in history is very varied and, in most cases, they were moving in small bands at different times, for different reasons and different means. Those who ended up in the Americas, Europe and the Arab world were mainly taken by force as slaves. Those from East Africa to the East, up to Australia and Asia were more voluntary or escapees, but most were later enslaved. Those that stayed in Africa were colonized by the Europeans and Arabs. Where-ever they went they ended up becoming slaves of one kind or another. Some called it colonization others called it civilization, religion, development or just slavery. Those who thought they were free, were in a designer slavery.

In this Bantu dispersal, the records are mainly oral and anthropological. There is ample evidence of these migrations in language and cultural similarities.

This presence of Bantus in Africa has created the illusion that they are the children of Ham. The Bible shows the genealogy of the Hamites in Gen 10:6 as: -

the *Cushite's* who are the Ethiopians,

the *Mizraim* who are the Egyptians,

the *Put* who are the Libyans and

the *Canaanites* who settled in Mesopotamia.

The Zondervan Compact Bible Dictionary description of Ham;

"He became the progenitor of the dark races; not the *Negroes*, but the Egyptians, Ethiopians, Libyans and Canaanites".

This description makes one wonder why they put *Negroes* which simply means black in Spanish. It came about when Spanish sailors saw black people and described them as black in color. In the above description, then "not the Negros" means "not the blacks" which is a misnomer since all the afore-mentioned races are black. Another way of looking at the statement would be; "progenitor of the dark races; not the blacks" Seriously? Earlier versions called them *Bantus*, which would have been a better description because the Bantus are black but not Hamites. What they did not tell us; who are the Blacks or Negroes.

So far, we can conclusively say,

- all Africans are Hamites,

- all Hamites are black (even the Canaanites),
- Not all black people are Africans,

We know: -

- Bantus are black
- Bantus are not Hamites

Therefore,

Bantus Are Not Africans

They are either the children of Japheth or Shem.

In the genealogy of Japheth, we know they settled in the low lands to the North of the Mediterranean Sea and the North East to Asia. This is present day Europe, and Asia. The inhabitants are white or pale and there is no major migration to Africa except for explores adventurers and economic exploiters. The only notable migration to Africa is that of the Boers of South Africa. These are Dutch farmers who settled in South Africa. They did not migrate from Europe through the land bridge, but through the sea route. They are still there as a distinct race of white people.

The Shemites are the neighbors of the Egyptians and they were in constant contact because of trade and migration. There are many instances recorded in the

Bible and other books of the children of Israel travelling to Egypt and staying for long periods either as guests or slaves. The history of the Shemites is well documented in the Bible. The most famous in this family are Abraham, Ishmael, Isaac, Esau and Jacob.

After the dispersal of the people at the tower of babel, the Most High was silent for a while until He started interacting with Abraham of the lineage of Shem. Abraham is also on record to have travelled to Egypt with his wife Sarah. He stayed awhile and taught them many disciplines like astrology and mathematics. He is alleged to have been a master of many crafts passed to him by his ancestors especially Methuselah. His wife Sarah is also alleged to have been among the four most beautiful women ever. Her beauty enamored the pharaoh, and Abraham left Egypt with much substance. During his interaction with God he got two sons Ishmael and Isaac.

Ishmael whom he got through his wife's Egyptian handmaid became prominent and became the father of the twelve princes. He is referred to as the child of the flesh. The Ishmaelites as they are called, are still present in Mesopotamia.

Isaac whom he got through his wife Sarah was the child of promise from God and he ended up being the carrier of God's promise to Abraham. He was the father of Esau and Jacob.

Esau was the eldest twin son of Isaac, but by a twist of fate and carelessness he lost the firstborn's birth-right and blessing to his younger brother. He is the father of the Edomite's. They are characterized as being red, not black.

Jacob was Isaac's younger son who through divine intervention and his elder brothers' carelessness, ended up getting the firstborn's birth-right and blessings. After encounter with God, his name was changed to Israel and he became the father of the twelve tribes of Israel. As mentioned earlier, after the dispersal of 135 C.E. they were in diaspora until the formation of the state of Israel in 1948. The main group in Israel currently is the Ashkenazi Jews who occupied Israel in 1948. Their lineage to the twelve sons of Israel is not clear but will be discussed later.

We have similarities between the Israelites and the Bantus and we will compare them with one Bantu group, the Gikuyu of Kenya;

- The Israelite God is invisible, so also is the Gikuyu God

- The Israelites are monotheist like the Gikuyu

- During the exodus, the presence of the Israelite God was manifested in a cloud by day and fire at night, the Gikuyu God was manifested by the snow cap on top of Mt. Kenya (Kirinyaga)

- The Israelites have a coming-of-age-ceremony known as Bar or Bat mitzva, while the Gikuyu have organized teachings to guide initiates into their new stage of responsibility known as Kirira

- The Israelites circumcise their young boys at age 8 days, the Gikuyu circumcise theirs into adulthood

- The Israelites were a polygamous people, so also were the Gikuyu people

- The Israelites were known to offer animal sacrifice to God, the same as the Gikuyu

- The genealogy of the Israelites is through the father, the same with the Gikuyu

These are only similarities from one Bantu group. When all known Bantu groups are considered, more similarities in language and culture are evident. With these many close similarities, there is need to investigate the relationship further.

*In this chapter we have established the Bantus or Negroes are not Hamites. They are not the children of Ham. We have not established a link to the children of Japheth – the Europeans and Asians. This leaves us with only one possible link that looks promising. And that is in the house of Shem – **the Israelites**.*

Chapter 5

THE SHEM - ISRAELITE CONNECTION

As we go through the bible, it becomes apparent, it is set to tell the story of the Hebrew Israelites. God set out to have the children of Noah re-populate the earth and the children of Israel to bless the earth.

From the onset, God set very clear guidelines on His relationship with the children of Israel and they accepted the blessings that came with the covenant they entered. The children of Israel also knew the consequences of not fulfilling the terms of the covenant. If they obeyed the terms they would be blessed, but if they disobeyed they would suffer the consequences of their disobedience.

Blessings and Curses

We learned earlier the genealogy of the children of Shem who are known as Shemites or Semites. Before we embark on the house of Israel, we will do some housekeeping in the house of Noah. He was the father of the three sons whose children we are dealing with. Sometimes we disregard patriarchal declarations in the family tree with dire consequences. We assume the instructions given by the patriarch do not carry weight. Let me whisper to you: Our people took those declarations seriously. If the old man declares something on his children, it is taken as a command. The only escape is to defy him when he dies and before he is buried. Otherwise they got stuck with the command for life or break it thereafter at their peril. It is whispered that those who have ever broken some of these commands had their children born lame, miscarriages or such other serious calamities in their lineage.

In the case of Noah, we see him taking the same actions. Noah became inebriated by his wine and exposed his nakedness. His youngest son Ham, the father of Canaan, saw the nakedness of his father and told his brothers outside. His brothers approached backwards and covered their father's naked body with a garment. When he sobered up, he knew what had happened!

Then he said, Gen 9:25 -27; "Cursed be Canaan; a servant of servants shall he be unto his brethren. And he said, Blessed be the Lord God of Shem; and Canaan shall be his servant. God shall enlarge Japheth, and he shall dwell in the tents of Shem; and Canaan shall be his servant."

It is with some interest we note that he cursed his grandson Canaan and not his son who was guilty of the indiscretion. The other sons of Noah were blessed with a twist. Japheth would be enlarged (made rich) and also, 'live in the tents of Shem'. The question arises, is it because Japheth would not be able to pitch his tents, after all he had just been blessed with enlargement or would Shem accommodate him out of his largesse, or because the Shemites would be absent and Japhetites would just move in. These are serious blessings and curses that we must keep in mind as we explore the families of the sons of Noah.

Shem's family settled in Mesopotamia after the dispersal of Gen 11:8. Hams family settled in North Africa except Canaan who settled in Mesopotamia against their allocation. Japheth and his children settled in Europe and Asia. The allocation of where to settle for the three families of the sons of Noah, was done by lot. They settled where they won, and it was enforceable.

From Shem, we jump to Abram who was to become Abraham. He was settled in Ur of the Chaldeans. This is Babylon or present- day Iraq. The Most High relocated him to Canaan. We note that God established a relationship with Abram that will be played out to the end of the age. He promised him the following in,

Gen 17:4-8;

*"As for me, behold, my covenant is with thee, and thou shalt be a **father of many nations**. Neither shall thy name any more be called Abram, but thy name shall be Abraham; for a father of many nations have I made thee. And I will make thee exceeding fruitful, and I will make nations of thee, and kings shall come out of thee. And I will establish my covenant between me and thee and thy seed after thee in their generations **for an everlasting covenant**, to be a God unto thee, and to thy seed after thee. And I will give unto thee, and to thy seed after thee, the land wherein thou art a stranger, **all the land of Canaan, for an everlasting possession**; and I will be their God."*

The sign was to be in the flesh, through **circumcision as an everlasting covenant.** God promised Abraham a son even in his old age. Sarah his wife was skeptical because of her advanced age and contrived to have Abraham get a son through her hand-maid. This arrangement produced Ishmael, but God said to Abraham in,

Genesis 17:15 -19;

"And God said unto Abraham, As for Sarai thy wife, thou shalt not call her name Sarai, but Sarah shall her

name be. And I will bless her, and give thee a son also of her: yea, I will bless her, and she shall be a mother of nations; kings of people shall be of her. Then Abraham fell upon his face, and laughed, and said in his heart, Shall a child be born unto him that is an hundred years old? and shall Sarah, that is ninety years old, bear? And Abraham said unto God, O that Ishmael might live before thee! And God said, Sarah thy wife shall bear thee a son indeed; and thou shalt call his name Isaac: and I will establish my covenant with him for an **everlasting covenant***, and* **with his seed after him***."*

Abraham became the father of Ishmael and Isaac. This is the second time Sarah is missing the script. Not following the instructions of the Most High brings strife. Abraham was promised a son by his wife Sarah. First, she snickered at the impossibility, cause of the deadness of her womb. Then she contrives a scheme to assist the Most High by giving her hand-maid to Abraham in order to get a son through her. That side arrangement brought problems that are still felt today. Ishmael was the product and he became the father of the twelve Ishmaelite princes as they are called to this day. He was referred to as the son of the flesh. The product of Abraham and Sarah was Isaac. He was referred to as the child of promise. This is because God promised Abraham this son through Sarah.

Isaac took Rebekah as wife. Gen 25:21 -23;

"And Isaac intreated the Lord for his wife, because she was barren: and the Lord was intreated of him, and Rebekah his wife conceived. And the children struggled together within her; and she said, If it be so, why am I thus? And she went to enquire of the Lord. And the Lord said unto her, Two nations are in thy womb, and two manner of people shall be separated from thy bowels; and the one people shall be stronger than the other people; and the elder shall serve the younger."

Isaac had two sons through his wife Rebekah, Esau and Jacob. It was apparent the house of Esau and Jacob would always be at war. Later Esau would sell his birthright to Jacob at the cost of a morsel of food.

Isaac bequeathed the first-born's blessing to his second born son as earlier shown in chapter 3. This miffed Esau and he planned to harm his brother Jacob, but his mother Rebekah knew. She organized with her husband Isaac how to get Jacob away.

Gen 28:1-4;

"And Isaac called Jacob, and blessed him, and charged him, and said unto him, Thou shalt not take a wife of the

daughters of Canaan. Arise, go to Padanaram, to the house of Bethuel thy mother's father; and take thee a wife from thence of the daughters of Laban thy mother's brother.

And God Almighty bless thee, and make thee fruitful, and multiply thee, that thou mayest be a multitude of people; And give thee the blessing of Abraham, to thee, and to thy seed with thee; that thou mayest inherit the land wherein thou art a stranger, which God gave unto Abraham."

He left Beersheba and went towards Haran. He stayed at a place all night. And he took a stone and put it at his head. He dreamt of a ladder to heaven. We read in, Genesis 28:13-15;

"And, behold, the Lord stood above it, and said, I am the Lord God of Abraham thy father, and the God of Isaac: the land whereon thou liest, to thee will I give it, and to thy seed; And thy seed shall be as the dust of the earth, and thou shalt spread abroad to the west, and to the east, and to the north, and to the south: and in thee and in thy seed shall all the families of the earth be blessed. And, behold, I am with thee, and will keep thee in all places whither thou goest, and will bring thee again into this land; for I will not leave thee, until I have

done that which I have spoken to thee of."

Jacob begat sons and daughters through his wives Leah and Rachel who were sisters and their maids Bilhah and Zilpah. On his way back home, his name was changed to Israel as we

read in, Gen 32:24-28;

"And Jacob was left alone; and there wrestled a man with him until the breaking of the day. And when he saw that he prevailed not against him, he touched the hollow of his thigh; and the hollow of Jacob's thigh was out of joint, as he wrestled with him. And he said, Let me go, for the day breaketh. And he said, I will not let thee go, except thou bless me. And he said unto him, What is thy name? And he said, Jacob. And he said, Thy name shall be called no more Jacob, but Israel: for as a prince hast thou power with God and with men, and hast prevailed."

Jacob's encounter with God started before he was born. When his mother enquired of the LORD why there was turmoil in her womb, she got the answer most mothers would not want to hear. Her children would fight each other, and one would serve the other. After Jacob left home to stay with his uncle Laban, he continued being the object of God's favor. Every time they had a discrepancy with his uncle about livestock he would always prevail. As indicated earlier the Most High chose the children of Noah to repopulate the earth after the flood according to Gen 9:1 but the house of Shem carried a special blessing to be enacted through the children of Israel.

Israel had twelve sons through his two wives who were sisters and their two maids. They were:

1.   LEAH – Reuben, Simeon, Levi, Judah, Issachar, Zebulun
2.   BILHA (Rachel's Handmaid) - Dan, Naphtali
3.   ZILPAH (Leah's handmaid) – Gad, Asher
4.   RACHEL- Joseph, Benjamin

The families of the twelve sons, became the twelve tribes of Israel, and they dwelt in the land of Canaan. Israel loved Joseph the most for he was the son of his old age. This made most of his other brothers envy him. The brothers planned to kill him, but Reuben convinced them to throw him in a pit. Later Judah organized, and they sold him to Ishmaelite merchants headed for Egypt. They told their father that Joseph had been killed by wild animals.

In Egypt Joseph rose from the position of a slave to one of the Government officials and became pharaoh's second in command. This was because he interpreted the pharaohs dream of an impending season of plenty followed by a famine season and the solution. During the severe famine, Egypt had ample food as overseen by Joseph.

Now there was also a famine in the land of Canaan and his family came to buy food. The family of Israel was reunited, and the Pharaoh learning of this invited them to stay. The stay lasted 430 years (Exodus 12:40). The family of Israel that came to Egypt were 70 and they became fruitful and increased abundantly and were mighty in the land. Now there arose a new king over Egypt who knew not Joseph. He planned and succeeded enslaving the children of Israel.

To end their slavery God used Moses. After a lot of struggle and calamities released over Egypt by the Most High they were finally free. They left on an overland journey headed to the land of Canaan promised to them by God. They were about six hundred thousand men (Exodus:12-38), besides women and children. A mixed multitude went up with them also. This means they could have been over two million. A journey that would have taken less than one month took forty years. Several things happened in this journey. The most important was that God led, provided and stayed with them. They left

Egypt disorganized and unprepared but became a nation. They established an organized leadership, judiciary and a well-trained standing army.

In the third month after the children of Israel left Egypt, they came to the Wilderness of Sinai. They stayed in the wilderness for forty years. Here the LORD gave the children of Israel instructions to live by. They are variously known as the ten commandments or the Law of Moses.

It is important to know that Moses was the servant and God Himself gave the instructions. The law is the law of YHWH.

Ex 19:5-7;

"Now therefore, if ye will obey my voice indeed, and keep my covenant, then ye shall be a peculiar treasure unto me above all people: for all the earth is mine: And ye shall be unto me a kingdom of priests, and an holy nation. These are the words which thou shalt speak unto the children of Israel. And Moses came and called for the elders of the people, and laid before their faces all these words which the Lord commanded him."

The Ten Commandments given were structured to govern the relationship between the children of Israel and their God, and between oneself and others, and for the conduct of oneself. These laws formed the basis of all their laws and statutes.

Moses who was not to cross the Jordan river into the promised land, prepared the children of Israel on how to access the blessings of the LORD and if they failed to follow His laws and statutes, the curses that they would face.

Deuteronomy 26:16-19;

"This day the Lord thy God hath commanded thee to do these statutes and judgments: thou shalt therefore keep and do them with all thine heart, and with all thy soul.

Thou hast avouched the Lord this day to be thy God, and to walk in his ways, and to keep his statutes, and his commandments, and his judgments, and to hearken unto his voice:

And the Lord hath avouched thee this day to be his peculiar people, as he hath promised thee, and that thou shouldest keep all his commandments; And to make thee high above all nations which he hath made, in praise, and in name, and in honor; and that thou mayest be a holy people unto the Lord thy God, as he hath spoken."

Moses commanded the people to proclaim the following curses upon which they would all answer Amen to each:

Deuteronomy 27:15-26;

Cursed be the man that maketh any graven or molten image, an abomination unto the Lord, the work of the hands of the craftsman, and putteth it in a secret place. Cursed be he that setteth light by his father or his mother. Cursed be he that removeth his neighbor's landmark;

Cursed be he that maketh the blind to wander out of the way; Cursed be he that perverteth the judgment of the stranger, fatherless, and widow;

Cursed be he that lieth with his father's wife; because he uncovereth his father's skirt; Cursed be he that lieth with any manner of beast; Cursed be he that lieth with his sister, the daughter of his father, or the daughter of his mother; Cursed be he that lieth with his mother in law;

Cursed be he that attacts his neighbor secretly; Cursed be he that taketh reward to slay an innocent person; Cursed be he that confirmeth not all the words of this law to do them;

Deuteronomy 28 is the culmination of the agreement God made with His children. It is what we call today "the satisfaction of" upon the out-come of fulfillment or lack thereof. The people had corporately proclaimed the curses (penalty) to befall them if they failed to satisfy the terms of the contract. The LORD had promised to keep

His end of the contract by blessing His children.

Moses details this contract as **blessings and curses.**
Deuteronomy 28:1-64.

"And it shall come to pass, if thou shalt hearken diligently unto the voice of the Lord thy God, to observe and to do all his commandments which I command thee this day, that the Lord thy God will set thee on high above all nations of the earth:

And all these blessings shall come on thee, and overtake thee, if thou shalt hearken unto the voice of the Lord thy God.

Blessed shalt thou be in the city, and blessed shalt thou be in the field.

Blessed shall be the fruit of thy body, and the fruit of thy ground, and the fruit of thy cattle, the increase of thy kine, and the flocks of thy sheep.

Blessed shall be thy basket and thy store.

Blessed shalt thou be when thou comest in, and blessed shalt thou be when thou goest out.

The Lord shall cause thine enemies that rise up against thee to be smitten before thy face: they shall come out against thee one way, and flee before thee seven ways.

The Lord shall command the blessing upon thee in thy storehouses, and in all that thou settest thine hand unto;

and he shall bless thee in the land which the Lord thy God giveth thee.

The Lord shall establish thee an holy people unto himself, as he hath sworn unto thee, if thou shalt keep the commandments of the Lord thy God, and walk in his ways.

And all people of the earth shall see that thou art called by the name of the Lord; and they shall be afraid of thee.

And the Lord shall make thee plenteous in goods, in the fruit of thy body, and in the fruit of thy cattle, and in the fruit of thy ground, in the land which the Lord sware unto thy fathers to give thee.

The Lord shall open unto thee his good treasure, the heaven to give the rain unto thy land in his season, and to bless all the work of thine hand: and thou shalt lend unto many nations,

and thou shalt not borrow.

And the Lord shall make thee the head, and not the tail; and thou shalt be above only, and thou shalt not be beneath; if that thou hearken unto the commandments of the Lord thy God, which I command thee this day, to observe and to do them:

And thou shalt not go aside from any of the words which I command thee this day, to the right hand, or to the left, to go after other gods to serve them.

But it shall come to pass, if thou wilt not hearken unto the voice of the Lord thy God, to observe to do all his commandments and his statutes which I command thee this day; that all these curses shall come upon thee, and overtake thee:

Cursed shalt thou be in the city, and cursed shalt thou be in the field.

Cursed shall be thy basket and thy store.

Cursed shall be the fruit of thy body, and the fruit of thy land, the increase of thy cattle, and the flocks of thy sheep.

Cursed shalt thou be when thou comest in, and cursed shalt thou be when thou goest out.

The Lord shall send upon thee cursing, vexation, and rebuke, in all that thou settest thine hand unto for to do, until thou be destroyed, and until thou perish quickly; because of the wickedness of thy doings, whereby thou hast forsaken me.

The Lord shall make the pestilence cleave unto thee, until he have consumed thee from off the land, whither thou goest to possess it.

The Lord shall smite thee with a consumption, and with a fever, and with an inflammation, and with an extreme *burning, and with the sword, and with blasting, and with mildew; and they shall pursue thee until thou perish.*

And thy heaven that is over thy head shall be brass, and the earth that is under thee shall be iron.

The Lord shall make the rain of thy land powder and dust: from heaven shall it come down upon thee, until thou be destroyed.

The Lord shall cause thee to be smitten before thine enemies: thou shalt go out one way against them, and flee seven ways before them: and shalt be removed into all the kingdoms of the earth.

And thy carcase shall be meat unto all fowls of the air, and unto the beasts of the earth, and no man shall fray them away.

The Lord will smite thee with the botch of Egypt, and with the hemorrhoids, and with the scab, and with the itch, whereof thou canst not be healed.

The Lord shall smite thee with madness, and blindness, and astonishment of heart:

And thou shalt grope at noonday, as the blind gropeth in darkness, and thou shalt not prosper in thy ways: and thou shalt be only oppressed and spoiled evermore, and no man shall save thee.

Thou shalt betroth a wife, and another man shall lie with

her: thou shalt build an house, and thou shalt not dwell therein: thou shalt plant a vineyard, and shalt not gather the grapes thereof.

Thine ox shall be slain before thine eyes, and thou shalt not eat thereof: thine ass shall be violently taken away from before thy face, and shall not be restored to thee: thy sheep shall be given unto thine enemies, and thou shalt have none to rescue them.

Thy sons and thy daughters shall be given unto another people, and thine eyes shall look, and fail with longing for them all the day long; and there shall be no might in thine hand.

The fruit of thy land, and all thy labors, shall a nation which thou knowest not eat up; and thou shalt be only oppressed and crushed always:

So that thou shalt be mad for the sight of thine eyes which thou shalt see.

The Lord shall smite thee in the knees, and in the legs, with a sore botch that cannot be healed, from the sole of thy foot unto the top of thy head.

The Lord shall bring thee, and thy king which thou shalt set over thee, unto a nation which neither thou nor thy fathers have known; and there shalt thou serve other gods, wood and stone.

And thou shalt become an astonishment, a proverb, and a byword, among all nations whither the Lord shall lead thee.

Thou shalt carry much seed out into the field, and shalt gather but little in; for the locust shall consume it.

Thou shalt plant vineyards, and dress them, but shalt neither drink of the wine, nor gather the grapes; for the worms shall eat them.

Thou shalt have olive trees throughout all thy coasts, but thou shalt not anoint thyself with the oil; for thine olive shall cast his fruit.

Thou shalt beget sons and daughters, but thou shalt not enjoy them; for they shall go into captivity.

All thy trees and fruit of thy land shall the locust consume.

The stranger that is within thee shall get up above thee very high; and thou shalt come down very low.

He shall lend to thee, and thou shalt not lend to him: he shall be the head, and thou shalt be the tail.

Moreover all these curses shall come upon thee, and shall pursue thee, and overtake thee, till thou be destroyed; because thou hearkenedst not unto the voice of the Lord thy God, to keep his commandments and his statutes which he commanded thee:

And they shall be upon thee for a sign and for a wonder, and upon thy seed for ever.

Because thou serves not the Lord thy God with joyfulness, and with gladness of heart, for the abundance of all things;

Therefore shalt thou serve thine enemies which the Lord shall send against thee, in hunger, and in thirst, and in nakedness, and in want of all things: and he shall put a yoke of iron upon thy neck, until he have destroyed thee.

The Lord shall bring a nation against thee from far, from the end of the earth, as swift as the eagle flieth; a nation whose tongue thou shalt not understand;

A nation of fierce countenance, which shall not regard the person of the old, nor shew favour to the young:

And he shall eat the fruit of thy cattle, and the fruit of thy land, until thou be destroyed: which also shall not leave thee either corn, wine, or oil, or the increase of thy kine, or flocks of thy sheep, until he have destroyed thee.

And he shall besiege thee in all thy gates, until thy high and fenced walls come down, wherein thou trustedst, throughout all thy land: and he shall besiege thee in all thy gates throughout all thy land, which the Lord thy God hath given thee.

And thou shalt eat the fruit of thine own body, the flesh

of thy sons and of thy daughters, which the Lord thy God hath given thee, in the siege, and in the straitness, wherewith thine enemies shall distress thee:

So that the man that is tender among you, and very delicate, his eye shall be evil toward his brother, and toward the wife of his bosom, and toward the remnant of his children which he shall leave:

So that he will not give to any of them of the flesh of his children whom he shall eat: because he hath nothing left him in the siege, and in the straitness, wherewith thine enemies shall distress thee in all thy gates.

The tender and delicate woman among you, which would not adventure to set the sole of her foot upon the ground for delicateness and tenderness, her eye shall be evil toward the husband of her bosom, and toward her son, and toward her daughter,

And toward her young one that cometh out from between her feet, and toward her children which she shall bear: for she shall eat them for want of all things secretly in the siege and straitness, wherewith thine enemy shall distress thee in thy gates.

If thou wilt not observe to do all the words of this law that are written in this book, that thou mayest fear this glorious and fearful name, The Lord Thy God;

Then the Lord will make thy plagues wonderful, and the plagues of thy seed, even great plagues, and of long continuance, and sore sicknesses, and of long continuance.

Moreover he will bring upon thee all the diseases of Egypt, which thou wast afraid of; and they shall cleave unto thee.

Also every sickness, and every plague, which is not written in the book of this law, them will the Lord bring upon thee, until thou be destroyed.

And ye shall be left few in number, whereas ye were as the stars of heaven for multitude; because thou wouldest not obey the voice of the Lord thy God.

And it shall come to pass, that as the Lord rejoiced over you to do you good, and to multiply you; so the Lord will rejoice over you to destroy you, and to bring you to nought; and ye shall be plucked from off the land whither thou goest to possess it.

And the Lord shall scatter thee among all people, from the one end of the earth even unto the other; and there thou shalt serve other gods, which neither thou nor thy fathers have known, even wood and stone.

And among these nations shalt thou find no ease, neither shall the sole of thy foot have rest: but the Lord shall give thee there a trembling heart, and failing of eyes, and sorrow of mind:

And thy life shall hang in doubt before thee; and thou shalt fear day and night, and shalt have none assurance of thy life:

In the morning thou shalt say, Would God it were even! and at even thou shalt say, Would God it were morning! for the fear of thine heart wherewith thou shalt fear, and for the sight of thine eyes which thou shalt see.

*And the Lord shall bring thee into Egypt again with ships, by the way whereof I spake unto thee, Thou shalt see it no more again: and there ye shall be sold unto your enemies for bondmen and bondwomen, and no man shall **buy you**."*

Shortly thereafter Moses passed on to join his ancestors. Before passing on he admonished the children of Israel thus,

Deuteronomy 31:27-29;

"For I know thy rebellion, and thy stiff neck: behold, while I am yet alive with you this day, ye have been rebellious against the Lord; and how much more after my death?

Gather unto me all the elders of your tribes, and your officers, that I may speak these words in their ears, and

call heaven and earth to record against them.

For I know that after my death ye will utterly corrupt yourselves, and turn aside from the way which I have commanded you; and evil will befall you in the latter days; because ye will do evil in the sight of the Lord, to provoke him to anger through the work of your hands."

The children of Israel led by Joshua, and after warring and defeating the inhabitants of Canaan, went forth and possessed the land. The lord was with them and prospered them in all ways. Israel served the Lord all the days of Joshua, and all the days of the elders who outlived Joshua, who had known all the works of the Lord which He had done for Israel.

Before passing on Joshua warned the children of Israel against interacting with the Canaanites but to drive them out.

Joshua 23:11-13;

"Take good heed therefore unto yourselves, that ye love the Lord your God. Else if ye do in any wise go back, and cleave unto the remnant of these nations, even these that remain among you, and shall make marriages with them, and go in unto them, and they to you: Know for a certainty that the Lord your God will no more drive out any of these nations from before you; but they shall be

snares and traps unto you, and scourges in your sides, and thorns in your eyes, until ye perish from off this good land which the Lord your God hath given you."

Some of the tribes failed to drive out the inhabitants of the land. They include Manasseh, Ephraim, Zebulun, Asher, Naphtali and Dan.

Despite all these warnings the children of Israel fell into the trap of integrating with their neighbors, thereby failing to honor the covenant.

Judges 2:1-4;

"And an angel of the Lord came up from Gilgal to Bochim, and said, I made you to go up out of Egypt, and have brought you unto the land which I sware unto your fathers; and I said, I will never break my covenant with you.

And ye shall make no league with the inhabitants of this land; ye shall throw down their altars: but ye have not obeyed my voice: why have ye done this?

Wherefore I also said, I will not drive them out from before you; but they shall be as thorns in your sides, and their gods shall be a snare unto you.

And it came to pass, when the angel of the Lord spake these words unto all the children of Israel, that the people lifted up their voice, and wept."

Judges 2:10-12;

"And also all that generation were gathered unto their fathers: and there arose another generation after them, which knew not the Lord, nor yet the works which he had done for Israel. And the children of Israel did evil in the sight of the Lord, and served Baalim: And they forsook the Lord God of their fathers, which brought them out of the land of Egypt, and followed other gods, of the gods of the people that were round about them, and bowed themselves unto them, and provoked the Lord to anger."

It seems the Israelites failed to teach their children the precept of spiritual transference as in

Proverbs 22:6;

"Train up a child in the way he should go: and when he is old, he will not depart from it."

Judges 2:14-23;

"And the anger of the Lord was hot against Israel, and he delivered them into the hands of spoilers that spoiled them, and he sold them into the hands of their enemies round about, so that they could not any longer stand before their enemies. Whithersoever they went out, the hand of the Lord was against them for evil, as the Lord had said, and as the Lord had sworn unto them: and they were greatly distressed. Nevertheless the Lord raised up

judges, which delivered them out of the hand of those that spoiled them. And yet they would not hearken unto their judges, but they went a whoring after other gods, and bowed themselves unto them: they turned quickly out of the way which their fathers walked in, obeying the commandments of the Lord; but they did not so. And when the Lord raised them up judges, then the Lord was with the judge, and delivered them out of the hand of their enemies all the days of the judge: for it repented the Lord because of their groanings by reason of them that oppressed them and vexed them. And it came to pass, when the judge was dead, that they returned, and corrupted themselves more than their fathers, in following other gods to serve them, and to bow down unto them; they ceased not from their own doings, nor from their stubborn way. And the anger of the Lord was hot against Israel; and he said, Because that this people hath transgressed my covenant which I commanded their fathers, and have not hearkened unto my voice; I also will not henceforth drive out any from before them of the nations which Joshua left when he died: That through them I may prove Israel, whether they will keep the way of the Lord to walk therein, as their fathers did keep it, or not. Therefore the Lord left those nations, without driving them out hastily; neither delivered he them into the hand of Joshua."

After the times of the Judges the children of Israel demanded their prophet Samuel, who was the last of the judges install for them a king in line with other nations. This was another way of assimilating the ways of other nations. They had already adopted their neighbors' gods, standards and practices, and now they wanted to adopt their ways of governance. The LORD was willing for the children of Israel to have a king, one who walked with the LORD, but their sin was wanting a king like all other nations. As in the times of the judges when they were faithful the LORD blessed them and when they were unfaithful He chastised them. The pinnacle of their rise was during the rule of king David and his son Solomon.

After the death of Solomon, his son Rehoboam led the split of Israel into two kingdoms, the North with ten tribes led by Jeroboam of the tribe of Ephraim, and the South with the tribe of Judah, Benjamin and Levi led by Rehoboam. The North was headquartered at Samaria while the South at Jerusalem. The two had different relations with the Most High. Jeroboam introduced Idol worship. The North with all their 20 kings was eviler in the eyes of the LORD. The LORD removed them from the land through the Assyrians who invaded in 772 B.C.E., took control of the North and most of them captive. Their fate thereafter is not clear and to date they are referred to as the lost 10 tribes of Israel.

The southern kingdom ruled by descendants of David did not fare much better, of their 20 kings eight were considered righteous and destroyed idols, but the last three were wicked. This saw the Babylonians exert tribute on Judah from 605 B.C.E., suffer deportations in 597 B.C.E., 586 B.C.E. and 581 B.C.E. After 70 years in captivity there arose a new king in Persia after the Babylonian king Nebuchadnezzar, his name was Cyrus. At the behest of the LORD, Cyrus released the captives of the Southern kingdom to go back to rebuild the Temple. One thing to note during their captivity there was always a king in Jerusalem of the lineage of David. This was to honor Gods promise to David of a perpetual Kingdom. It took the returnees three waves over a span of 100 years to finally return home.

The first wave of Jewish exiles returns to Jerusalem around 536 B.C.E., and with the permission of King Cyrus of Persia, begins to rebuild the Temple. The third wave of Jewish exiles returns to Jerusalem around 445 B.C.E. and, under Nehemiah the walls of Jerusalem were rebuilt. However, a significant number choose to stay 'in exile'. In 167 B.C.E the Temple is defiled by Antiochus IV Epiphanes (Greek), who sacrifices a sow on the altar and halts the Temple worship. Three years later Judas Maccabeus liberates and cleanses the Temple. The Hasmoneans rule Israel until the Roman invasion.

In 63 B.C.E, the Roman general Pompey conquered the land of Israel, ended the Hasmonean (Greek) state and brought Palestine into the Roman Empire. In the year 66 C.E., Florus, the last Roman procurator, stole vast quantities of silver from the Temple. The outraged Jewish masses rioted and wiped out the small Roman garrison stationed in Jerusalem. Cestius Gallus, the Roman ruler in neighboring Syria, sent in a larger force of soldiers. But the Jewish insurgents routed them as well. When the Romans returned, they had 60,000 heavily armed and highly professional troops. They launched their first attack against the Jewish state's most radicalized area, the Galilee in the north. The Romans vanquished the Galilee, and an estimated 100,000 Jews were killed or sold into slavery. During the summer of 70 C.E., the Romans breached the walls of Jerusalem, and initiated an orgy of violence and destruction. The second Temple was destroyed by the Romans.

Approximately one million Jews were killed and most of the survivors were sold into slavery or scattered into the nations. However, a small remnant of Jews remained in the Land throughout the dispersion.

When Hadrian first became the Roman emperor in 118 C.E., he was sympathetic to the Jews. He allowed them to return to Jerusalem and granted permission for the rebuilding of their Holy Temple. The Jews' expectations rose as they made organizational and financial preparations to rebuild the temple. Hadrian quickly went back on his word and ordered the site of the Temple to be moved from its original location. He also began deporting Jews to North Africa. The Jews rebelled under Bar-Kokhba and fighting ensued. The final battle of the war took place in Bethar, Bar-Kokhba's headquarters, which housed both the Sanhedrin (Jewish High Court) and the home of the Nasi (leader). Bethar was a vital military stronghold because of its strategic location on a mountain ridge overlooking both the Valley of Sorek and the important Jerusalem-Bet Guvrin Road. Thousands of Jews fled to Bethar, for refuge during the war. In 135 C.E., Hadrian's army besieged Bethar and on the 9th of Av, the Jewish fast day commemorating the destruction of the first and second Holy Temples, the walls of Bethar fell. After a fierce battle, every Jew in Bethar was killed. Six days passed before the Romans allowed the Jews to bury their dead. They renamed Jerusalem 'Aelia Capitolina' and the land 'Syria Palestina' to eradicate the memory of the Jewish people there.

This was essentially the end of the ancient nation of Israel. The cause was not the strength of their opponents but their disobedience to God.

We have seen the choices given the children of Israel by their God. We have also seen their poor decision that led to their loss. Their main fault was their inability to pass on their culture that hinged on God to their progeny. The punishment that befell their children was the result.

Chapter 6

ISRAEL DISPERSED

In a last effort to reclaim Sovereignty after the defeat of 70 C.E., the children of Israel were completely routed out of their homeland by the Romans and forbidden to return. So, where are they?

Why and Where To?

As we have seen, the reason for the turbulent history of the nation of Israel, revolves around their relationship with God. The LORD makes it clear that their obedience will be rewarded with blessings and their disobedience with curses. Exodus 28 is very clear and detailed on the outcome of their behavior. Moses even laments that they will behave like they eventually did. All manner of tactics to keep them in obedience to the Most High were used. They even swore as a corporate body and accepted the consequences of their behavior in Joshua 8:30-35 as ordered by Moses in Deuteronomy 27:11. Gods' law was central, and when they were obedient and lived righteous lives, God blessed them and fought their battles, but they broke the law with impunity especially the first one, "thou shalt have no other God but Me". They aped their neighbors' ways of worshipping idols. This is exactly what the LORD predicted in,

Deuteronomy 31:14-18;

"And the Lord said unto Moses, Behold, thy days approach that thou must die: call Joshua, and present yourselves in the tabernacle of the congregation, that I may give him a charge. And Moses and Joshua went, and presented themselves in the tabernacle of the congregation.

And the Lord appeared in the tabernacle in a pillar of a cloud: and the pillar of the cloud stood over the door of the tabernacle.

And the Lord said unto Moses, Behold, thou shalt sleep with thy fathers; and this people will rise up, and go a whoring after the gods of the strangers of the land, whither they go to be among them, and will forsake me, and break my covenant which I have made with them.

Then my anger shall be kindled against them in that day, and I will forsake them, and I will hide my face from them, and they shall be devoured, and many evils and troubles shall befall them; so that they will say in that day, Are not these evils come upon us, because our God is not among us?

And I will surely hide my face in that day for all the evils

which they shall have wrought, in that they are turned unto other gods."

This eventually happened, and they were led into captivity and back severally over a period of over 900 years from around 772 B.C.E. to around 135 C.E. and are still in diaspora to date.

There are several instances of Israelites leaving their ancestral homeland to settle voluntarily or otherwise in foreign lands. It is recorded that even after returning home, some remnants are left behind in the foreign lands for various reasons.

The Israelite migrations started with Joseph, the 11th son of Jacob around 1700 B.C.E. After being sold by his brothers, he ended up in Egypt as a slave. He later became the second most powerful man in the land after the Pharaoh, because he interpreted the Pharaoh's dream about the coming plenty and famine. He also advised him on measures to take to safe-guard his people. The pharaoh made him overseer of all Egypt. We read in,

Genesis 41:56 – 42:3;

"And the famine was over all the face of the earth: and Joseph opened all the storehouses, and sold unto the Egyptians; and the famine waxed sore in the land of Egypt.

And all countries came into Egypt to Joseph for to buy corn; because that the famine was so sore in all lands. Now when Jacob saw that there was corn in Egypt, Jacob said unto his sons, Why do ye look one upon another? And he said, Behold, I have heard that there is corn in Egypt: get you down thither, and buy for us from thence; that we may live, and not die. And Joseph's ten brethren went down to buy corn in Egypt."

The house of Jacob was reunited with Joseph, and at the behest of the Pharaoh, settled in Egypt. What started as a trip to the market became a 430-year sojourn with slavery being included. It took the hand of God to free them from their oppressors through Moses in what was called the exodus. After a 40-year journey, they returned to their homeland in Canaan.

After they had settled in the promised land of Canaan they ended up in slavery again. This time it was not caused by a trip to the market but because of their disobedience to God. They were led into captivity by the Assyrians, Babylonians and Romans. By 135 C.E. the nation of Israel was virtually in diaspora. They were dispersed to the four corners of the earth.

So, **where are the Israelites today**?

This will be our challenge in this chapter. For a period of over 1800 years, from 135 C.E. there was no state of Israel. Then in 1948 the United Nations re-established the State of Israel in the promised land. This effort led by Britain allocated the land to people that were not vetted to be bona fide Israelites. More on this later.

After the dispersal of 135 C.E., the where about of the Israelites became unclear. It was as if there was a plan to blot out their existence completely. Several things to note in our quest to establish their where about; whenever there was a need to relocate from their homeland, for any reason, they always headed south. To Egypt.

The scriptures record many instances when they went to Egypt starting with their ancestors Abraham in Genesis 12:10;

"And there was a famine in the land: and Abram went down into Egypt to sojourn there; for the famine was grievous in the land."

Then came Isaac and we read in,

Genesis 26:1-2;

"And there was a famine in the land, beside the first famine that was in the days of Abraham. And Isaac went

unto Abimelech king of the Philistines unto Gerar. And the Lord appeared unto him, and said, Go not down into Egypt; dwell in the land which I shall tell thee of."

It's clear he intended to go to Egypt.

As mentioned earlier the house of Israel sojourned in Egypt for many years where they grew from 70 in number to become a nation. Then came the Messiah in, Mathew 2:13-14;

"And when they were departed, behold, the angel of the Lord appeareth to Joseph in a dream, saying, Arise, and take the young child and his mother, and flee into Egypt, and be thou there until I bring thee word: for Herod will seek the young child to destroy him. When he arose, he took the young child and his mother by night, and departed into Egypt"

During the prophetic ministry of the Messiah He prophesied the destruction of Jerusalem, and we read in Mathew 24: 15-16;

"When ye therefore shall see the abomination of desolation, spoken of by Daniel the prophet, stand in the holy place, (whoso readeth, let him understand:) Then let them which be in Judaea flee into the mountains."

The mountains He was speaking of are the Atlas Mountains in North Africa. To get there from Canaan they had to pass through Egypt. It makes sense to start the search where they were last seen. For the Jews, it has to be Egypt. The dispersal of the Israelites was foretold as we read in,

Deuteronomy 28:58;

"If thou wilt not observe to do all the words of this law that are written in this book, that thou mayest fear this glorious and fearful name, The Lord Thy God."

Verse 64;

"And the Lord shall scatter thee among all people, from the one end of the earth even unto the other; and there thou shalt serve other gods, which neither thou nor thy fathers have known, even wood and stone."

Verse 68;

"And the Lord shall bring thee into Egypt again with ships, by the way whereof I spake unto thee, Thou shalt see it no more again: and there ye shall be sold unto your enemies for bondmen and bondwomen, and no man shall buy you."

If you get lost while navigating, it's always prudent to return to your last known position and start again. In the case of Israelites, they were dispersed to the four corners of the earth! Those that escaped invasions in the Holy land, would head for Egypt. There are also accounts of others escaping Egyptian slavery before the Exodus. When it was apparent the Assyrian, Babylonian and Roman captivities were eminent some escaped to Africa, especially Egypt and Ethiopia. From all their captivities, the Israelites were scattered to all the corners of the earth. To trace their current location would require searching the whole earth. But we have two clues; Egypt as a staging area and the curse of them in Deuteronomy 28:68 stating, *"And the Lord shall bring thee into Egypt again with ships, by the way whereof I spake unto thee, Thou shalt see it no more again."*

It is in record that their enemies the Romans pursued the Jews to Egypt and they continued inland in Africa where the Romans had no power. In Africa, some disappeared North to the countries of the Maghreb, this being the Atlas Mountains Jesus advised them. Others went south towards Ethiopia, Sudan and beyond. Others disappeared west across the Sahara all the way to West Africa.

Another interesting point to note is they would be taken into Egypt with ships via the way where the LORD spoke to them. The LORD spoke to them at Mt. Sinai on their way from Egypt to the promised land during the Exodus. This is where He gave them the laws.

The LORD was telling them they would backtrack their Exodus route to Egypt. He was also telling them it would be to a far place where they would be taken in ships. From Canaan to Egypt there is no ocean, therefore no ships required. This Egypt being referred can't be their neighbor, but the bible usually interprets itself.

Deuteronomy 5:6;

" I am the Lord thy God, which brought thee out of the land of Egypt, from the house of bondage."

In verse 68, Egypt, is allegorically referring to house of bondage or slavery. This means they would go into slavery (house of bondage) with ships. The passage becomes clear; **they would be taken into slavery; their route would be through Mt. Sinai and Egypt to a far place requiring ships and they would not be coming back home**.

So, we will look for them in a far place from home, where they were enslaved and not in Canaan. In the later part of their main dispersion around 70 C.E., over one million Jews fled to Africa. Many of them ended up in the slave markets and others went further inland to the North, South and West. The cause of their penetrating deeper into Africa was an attempt to escape their enemies, mainly the Romans who routed them out of their homeland and pursued them. Around this dispersal the Romans held sway militarily in Egypt where they would have tarried, it was a Roman Province.

When trying to answer the question of the Israelite's whereabouts, one is often inclined to begin the search from the Holy Land. After their defeat by the Romans around 135 C.E., the state of Israel ceased to exist. The land was occupied by others. The occupiers were mainly from the neighboring Arab communities and Africans who laid claim to the virtually empty land. Others were settled there by the Romans to replace and blot out the memory of the Israelites. Some claimed the land was theirs before the Israelites routed them out after the exodus. Jerusalem, the main city of interest has been claimed over the years by the Hebrews, Muslims and even Christians.

After the 2nd world war ended in 1945, there was a sympathetic move to settle the Jews who it was alleged had been persecuted world-wide mostly for religious reasons. This clamor was fueled to its height by reports of Jews in German death camps perpetrated by Adolf Hitler. The proponents wanted the State of Israel to be established and many places were suggested including Africa. It is worthy of note that around 1945 and before, most of Africa was under colonialism from European powers. Parts of the middle East were also under their control. The area of Palestine happened to have been under the British.

The United Nations, led by Britain re-established the State of Israel in 1948. The short of it was, all Israelites could return home. The modus operadi did not establish who they were or where they were. It looks like there were underhand dealings that were designed to bring in the Jews from two main groups of people who call themselves the Ashkenazi Jews and Sephardi Jews. The Ashkenazi Jews came bodily from Eastern Europe and the Sephardi Jews from Western Europe.

Several questions arise from this arrangement;

- Why are these people calling themselves Jews? Anybody can convert and be a Jew, but a Hebrew Israelite is a blood descendent of Abraham, Isaac and Jacob;

- How come they are coming from only two locales in Europe? after the Israelite dispersal they went to all the corners of the earth;

- How come they did not re-emerge from Africa? The last time the Jews were seen they were disappearing into Africa not Europe, and

- the ten tribes of Israel scattered in Eurasia.
- As we saw in this chapter the LORD told them they were going into slavery and not coming back. Unless you want to doubt the LORD, then we must agree that those in Israel are not Israelites!
- Didn't we read in Genesis 10:1-3, "Now these are the generations of the sons of Noah, Shem, Ham, and Japheth: and unto them were sons born after the flood.

  The sons of **Japheth**; Gomer, and Magog, and Madai, and Javan, and Tubal, and Meshech, and Tiras.

  And the sons of Gomer; **Ashkenaz**, and Riphath, and Togarmah".

  Could this Ashkenaz the grandson of Japheth be the same as the Ashkenazi Jew in Israel? I wonder.
- In 1492 King Ferdinand and Queen Isabella of Spain, expelled all the Jews from Spain. They were the Sephardic Jews. Sephardi means Jews of Spain and Portugal. After they were expelled they ended up in North Africa.

  How come they re-emerged from Spain to

settle in Palestine in 1948?

- Did we not also read Noah blessing his children in Genesis 9:27;

"God shall enlarge Japheth, and he shall **dwell in the tents of Shem**; and **Canaan shall be his servant**".

Looks like the descendants of Japheth (Ashkenazi and Sephardi) are dwelling (living) in the tents (dwellings or houses) of Shem (Israelites). If that is the case then, it follows that the owners of the dwellings (Israelites) are absent! The Canaanites remaining in Canaan today work as servants in Israel. Remember these Canaanites were not even supposed to settle in Mesopotamia in the first place, but in Africa, but out of sedition they did and out of sedition they were routed out; now they are servants of Japheth like their ancestor Noah prophesied. Their father Ham and brothers told them they will be routed out by sedition. One of the meanings of sedition, is rebelling against authority. In this case, it means the occupation of Canaan was by a lie and they would be removed through deceit.

They prevented the bona-fide owners (Shemites) to settle, and they would be removed by equally unqualified or deceitful settlers.

The conclusion of this matter is straight forward. The Hebrew Israelites are not in Israel, maybe a few.

The current occupiers of Israel are either imposters or Jewish converts.

Another set of question needs to be answered. If you met a bona fide Hebrew Israelite, how would you know?

To answer this question, we first must establish why the true Hebrew Israelite is silent and if he is speaking, why won't we listen or hear?

To understand the Israelite, we look at his story and his story is basically what the bible is all about. The bible charts a path that is to be followed by them through teachings, prophesy and commandments. It's a book about God and His relationship with His children.

As we have read in Deuteronomy 28, the consequences of their disobedience would be catastrophic displacement. They disobeyed, and they were displaced or dispersed into the four corners of the earth.

Why the silence or amnesia?

Deuteronomy 32 is the Song of Moses that the LORD commanded Moses to speak to all Israel. In verse 26 (NKV) we read;

"I would have said, "I will dash them in pieces, ***I will make the memory of them to cease from among men".***

The LORD was of a mind to completely destroy His people, what saved them is in verse 27 (NKV)

"Had I not feared the wrath of the enemy, lest their adversaries should misunderstand, lest they should say, "Our hand is high; And it is not the Lord who has done all this."

He did not want the enemies to claim credit for this punishment.

We also noted in Chapter 5, the captivities by the Assyrian invasion of 722 B.C.E., the Babylonian in 597 - 535 B.C.E. and the Roman invasion of 70 C.E. which culminated with the fall of Bethar in 135 C.E., they renamed Jerusalem 'Aelia Capitolina' and the land 'Syria Palestina' **to eradicate the memory of the Jewish people**.

 From then on, the surviving Jews were on the run from their enemies. One of the ways you escape your enemies is to *hide your identity*. They had been involved in conflict for over 800 years. They were battle hardened and would overwhelm those who resisted their escape, but their enemies were powerful, persistent and held sway over most of the lands around the Middle East.

Another tactic to escape your enemies is to hide in plain sight. They would stay in small bands and hide in communities that *looked like themselves*. The local people would recognize them as foreigners, but their pursuers would not. Another tactic they would use is not to advertise who they were, by giving themselves a *new name or local one*. They would also learn a new language or corrupt their own. After many generations, the memory of their identity would fade.

It is therefore fair to conclude the following;

- the LORD turned His face from them;
- the powers that were, conspired to eradicate the memory of their existence;
- the victims hid their identity for safety; wherever they are, they have a new name or names and language;
- In general, they do not know their identity.

After the 1948 resettling of the Jews in Israel, wars started with the local 'Palestinians' who claimed ownership of the land. Thereafter the Egyptian president, acknowledged the Jews that left were black but came back white. What?!!

This is the first real evidence that the current occupiers of Israel are not Israelites. For the first time in modern history we get a clue of the color of the real **Israelites being black**. If anybody should know the Israelites, it must be the Egyptians. They are neighbors and the Israelites have spent considerable time in Egypt. This narrows our search to seek the Israelites, not as white people but as black people. This must be the biggest secret kept by the powers that are, to conspire to hide and replace a people for reasons that we must decipher. It shows the bible was right all along; the Israelites left and are not coming back, and others of the lineage of Japheth have replaced them by claiming to be Jews. We read in,

Revelation 2:9;

*"I know your works, tribulation, and poverty (but you are rich); and I know the **blasphemy** of those who say they are Jews and are not, but are a synagogue of Satan."*

Another clue just emerged, they face tribulation, are poor and the LORD knows the Jews in Israel are imposters. He also says they are rich, because in the coming dispensation they will own everything, including their enemies.

The conspiracy is pointing to the Europeans corporately. They are the ones who routed out the Israelites from their homeland, they even replaced them, they pursued them out of the territories they held sway, and in 1948 they planted imposters in Israel.

Since the time the Jews were routed out of their land, its more than 1800 years. It's enough time for people to change completely, forget their language, culture and even their identity. This is more so if there is a plot to hide history. The only people capable of this were the Europeans. They included the British, Portuguese, Romans, Spanish, Germans, etc. They are even recorded to have colluded in partitioning Africa and the rest of the world they had conquered. There is even evidence of the Catholic Church-read Rome, being in cahoots to subjugate people in the most atrocious ways. These included slavery, torture, murder, rape etc.

We know that over time people who are in perpetual captivity can lose their identity, more so their stock of knowledge. It behooves to point out that victors write the histories of their victims. I believe the successful disappearance of the Jews in Africa was two pronged:

First they were a people being pursued and they tried to hide their identity by changing their name and names. Their pursuers vowed to blot out their existence. In all these we should not forget the main determining factor; their relationship with God. He told them they would be dispersed if they disobeyed and it happened like it had happened before.

Since the disappearance of the Israelites was very well orchestrated and successful, we can't continue following their tracks. If a tracker follows tracks into a river or sand, the tracks disappear and the only way to continue is search for their exit or predict their destination and head there. For the Israelites their destination, part of the route they were to take and means of travel are all laid out in Deuteronomy 28:68. We know they disappeared mostly into Africa through Egypt, also Europe and Asia, from around 1600 B.C.E., when it is estimated the Israelites started facing difficulties in Egypt to their final dispersal of 135 C.E. We will try to find a community that suffered slavery, taken into slavery with ships and has a connection with Africa especially through Egypt, that is black and has hidden or forgotten its identity. Then we will back track it to Egypt or Canaan. When we look at it this way, it becomes very simple but almost outrageous. Looking in hindsight, the Israelites are hidden in plain sight.

Other than the Canaanites, and the Boers of South Africa, there is only one group of people that lives in areas not allocated to them during the Sons of Noah dispersal. This group does not even know it's race or nationality. Every group of people can be traced back to Noah and Sons. This group lives in areas not allocated to them during the dispersal of Noah's Sons. This group is worldwide. This group, wherever they call home, they are in forced migration, even though most don't know it. They have been enslaved as per Deuteronomy 28. If your thoughts have not yet coalesced to a specific group; let me help you. These are the victims of the infamous transatlantic slave trade and other forms of subjugation. They are black;

- went into or are still in slavery;
- taken into slavery with ships;
- they came from or through Africa;
- they do not know their identity;

You might ask, aren't they supposed to be all over the world? True, but this is only the traceable sample. From these we can backtrack them to Canaan and on the way, maybe pick up their relatives? Remember this saga is more than 3000 years old, from when Joseph was taken to Egypt to-date.

We have seen the Israelites left Israel and have not returned. This is further enforced by their neighbors who know the current occupiers of Israel are not genuine Israelites.

Chapter 7

QUEST

About three years ago a young black American accused "us Africans" of having sold "their people" into slavery. Having come from Africa I became guilty of a crime I was not even aware of. The young man quoted books written on the subject by African Americans, "who had even travelled to Africa for this quest". My defense that we were also in our own kind of slavery then, fell on deaf ears. This accusation disturbed me for a while and I decided to do my own research.

And seeking this answer is the culmination of this book.

In Search of My Ancestry

I was born in Kenya during a period referred to as the 'emergency period'. Kenyans were fighting the British colonizers for their independence. The British had come to Kenya as Government agents, Missionaries, Adventurers and Opportunists. Their settling in Kenya was sanctioned by their Government to appease political hangers on, military war returnees, and generally to populate the area with British economic exploiters who would steal from the country of its resources, in the guise of development. They forcibly took the prime farming land thereby denying us a source of liveli-hood. They instituted taxation to force our people to work for money, to pay the tax. This was a plan to force our people to seek employment from them. This provided them with slave labor for their farms, in the guise of employment.

These are the people who were supposed to have been trading in human cargo; while they themselves were virtual slaves. If we were guilty of this crime, how come I never heard of it from our people and especially how we benefitted selling our brothers.

In chapter 2, we laid the foundation of the origin of my people. The origin of the Gikuyu people is very sudden. A man and his wife suddenly emerge at a place known as 'Mukurwe-ini-wa-Nyagathanga' and starts a family now known as the Gikuyu tribe, with over ten million strong.

In chapter 4 we established that from Noah's sons, only Shem was a possible candidate as the father of the Bantus. We there after followed the Shem family to the Israelites, until they disappeared mainly into Africa and elsewhere.

We have established that my people the Kikuyu Bantu of Kenya are a black people of unknown ancestry linking them to the sons of Noah. We have seen that we reside in Africa, yet we are not Hamites because, we are not the children of Ham the progenitor of the Africans. The only people with close traits to the Bantus are the Hebrew Israelites.

We have also established that, the Hebrew Israelites started sojourning into Africa with Joseph son of Jacob around 1700 B.C.E. up to around 135 C.E., when Israel ceased to exist. That is a period of over 1800 years and the dates are approximated. After the final displacement of 135 B.C.E., the Israelites never returned to the holy land, and for all intents and purposes they are still in diaspora. The final dispersal was so well orchestrated that it's difficult to pursue this line of search further. They were systematically hunted and if caught, either killed or enslaved. Those that escaped hid themselves very well. It is estimated that millions of Jews fled into Africa or were forcibly taken. Africa and the world has the moral obligation to tell us what happened to the Children of Israel. Since they are silent the next best tactic is to search for a people who progressively appeared as the Israelites were disappearing. This group also needs to fit into the curses of Deuteronomy 28 and other features described in scripture and history.

The only group that fits most of these criterion is the **Bantu.**

The description of the Bantu as a people is usually described from a migratory or expansion point of view, not a point of origin or ancestry. In most Bantu languages, the name "BANTU" closely relates or translates to 'people' or 'the people'. Their emergence and expansion in west Africa and elsewhere is placed between 2000 B.C.E. and 1500 B.C.E. and continues to date. This is the approximate time the Israelites were sojourning into Africa. The timeline of these two incidences is too close to ignore. The Israelites are trying hard to disappear into Africa, and the Bantus, who did not have prior history, appears and starts rapidly migrating across Africa as if something was after them.

The Bantus are all over the world. They are known by many names, including Gikuyus of Kenya, African Americans, Blacks, Negroes of the Americas, Chagas of Tanzania, Lembas of Southern Africa, Ibos of Nigeria and many others depending on country. The question now arises did these people or part thereof experience the curses of Deuteronomy 28, and if so how do they connect with the now disappeared Israelites. There is also a lingering issue of the Jews in Palestine to be dealt with later.

In my quest, I went back in history as far as I could but, this quest was curtailed by scarcity of information of our origins. Our ancestors Gikuyu and his wife Mumbi, as we were told, emerged at a place called Mukurwe-ini-wa-Nyagathanga. The question was, where did they emerge out of? Where were they coming from? Why would they not pass on this information of their origins to their children? The Gikuyu people can recall their history about age group, family lineage and Governing group almost to Gikuyu himself, but nothing at all before Mukurwe-ini. It is my contention Gikuyu did not forget this important detail. It was deliberately omitted for a reason, and the reason is simple – to hide their whereabouts and identity from would be inquirers or pursuers. Does this sound familiar? It sure does. It happened with the Jews as they disappeared into Africa!

For Gikuyu and Mumbi to suddenly appear at Mukurwe-ini-wa-Nyagathaga out of nowhere, and hide their origin and names, looks to me like a people on the run. They were being pursued or they thought so. Also, not to forget they were grown people when they arrived for them to be referred as Gikuyu and his wife Mumbi. If they were man and wife, then they must have left their families somewhere. As I intimated in chapter 2, they must have escaped a catastrophic episode resulting in their running away or getting lost. Looks to me they escaped a military operation. This would explain their emerging. Once during military training, I was spotted by the 'enemy' and a chase ensued for several miles in sparsely vegetated savannah. What saved me from capture was; as I rounded a small bushy area on the animal path I was following, in front I saw a bigger thicket about 100 feet in diameter. It was a thicket of mature stinging nettle. I was temporary out of sight from my pursuers, so I plunged through the thicket headlong to the center where I emerged into a small clearing. My pursuers could not figure out where I had disappeared, I could say I emerged at the small clearing. It behooves me to point out my experience did not start at the small clearing, but elsewhere. All I had to do was stay put and endure the burn caused by the stinging nettle, until the 'enemy' gave up. It is my contention Gikuyu tried and very well succeeded, in hiding their identity and merged with the locals for a reason. And the reason is, to escape discovery from powerful enemies who they believed would be pursuing them. Those enemies must have been very powerful and with long memories. Also, the reason for the flight must have been important enough for posterity. That's why even as he was dying he never told his children their true origin in order to protect them. You can't reveal what you do not know! We need to know the powers that were there around that time and wanting to pursue others into Africa. It is apparent the ones being pursued were from without, that's why they were trying to hide within local communities who looked like them and were not in danger of being found out. Then they would wait out their enemies, until they gave up or forgot.

This is kind of obvious. Our people the Gikuyu are only 1600 miles South of Egypt, and around this time it was the Roman influenced campaigns that were pursuing Hebrew Israelites into Africa. Remember the Romans later colonized Somalia which is 600 miles to the North East.

Another intriguing fact is that of language and culture. To a keen researcher it's possible to fish out similarities amongst different Bantu groups, but if checked casually they are all different. I believe, one of the methods they used to disappear was to refrain from using their language and culture but learn local ones to disappear. They could also corrupt words to confuse the enemy. We saw this happening in Kenya during the struggle for independence, the freedom fighters called out to each other 'uma' meaning 'come out', but to conceal the message if heard by their enemies, the British colonizers, they would call out 'mau mau'. Even so, a lot of words and cultural practices are similar throughout the Bantu people.

Our people, the Agikuyu, are also of the Bantu group of people. I call them group because they are of no established race, for they are not Africans, Europeans or Asians. The origin of all races is the Sons of Noah. The Bantus are wide spread in Sub-Saharan Africa and many parts of the world. The history of the Bantu, when checked in any fora does not tell of their origin. It tells of the Bantu expansion. Several theories indicate the Bantu as a migrating people, mostly from West Africa towards Central Africa, then East and South. There is also supposed migration from North East Africa, Westwards and Southwards. It does not indicate their origin. Same story we saw with the Gikuyu people. The ancestry of the Bantu is shrouded with secrecy. A few of the groups in the Bantu band wagon can recall their sojourn from Mesopotamia and others Egypt. Some even recall being Hebrews; The Lemba of Southern and South Africa claim to be the Hebrew Israelite tribe of Levi. They are black; The Ibos of Nigeria claim they are the original Hebrews Israelites and migration of the Bantus started from them. They are black;

The Abayudaya of Uganda assert to be Hebrew Israelites of old. Abayudaya could be a corruption of people of Judah. ('Aba- prefix meaning 'the people' and 'yudaya' meaning Yudah). They are black;

The presence of Israelites in West Africa is also captured by the 1747 map of West Africa showing the Kingdom of Juda or Whidah above slave coast. It is also believed IBO or IGBO of Nigeria, is a corruption for HEBREW. Try to pronounce the two names rapidly, and the similarity is obvious. They are bantus and black;

 If you look at the Bantu migratory routes, you begin to wander, where were they going? If it was due to population pressure then you would expect large concentrations of people, but until modern times most of these areas were sparsely populated. It looks like they were migrating in small bands mostly into the interior of Africa. What were they escaping from, if not their enemies?

We have been led to believe that Jews are white, this is not true for they are black. It has been orchestrated to blot out the identity of the true Hebrew Israelites.

Until modern times skin color was not an issue, but God knowing that a time was coming when His children would need an assurance of who they were, He left them clues and hints all over the scriptures about this crucial piece of information.

- In Genesis 42:8;

  "And Joseph knew his brethren, but they knew not him."

  Why? Because he looked like the EGYPTIANS and they were black.

- In Exodus 2:6;

  "And when she had opened it, she saw the child: and, behold, the babe wept. And she had compassion on him, and said, this is one of the Hebrews' children."

  Verse 10;

  "And the child grew, and she brought him unto Pharaoh's daughter, and he became her son. And she called his name Moses: and she said, Because I drew him out of the water."

  Moses was able to live in the palace and pass as Egyptian because he was black like them.

- In Exodus 2:19; *"And they said, An Egyptian delivered us out of the hand of the shepherds, and also drew water enough for us, and watered the flock."*

These were Kenite shepherds and would have known Egyptians are a black people. If it was a matter of dressing, then they would have referred of Moses as a white man in Egyptian dress.

- The flight into Egypt is a biblical event described in the Gospel of Matthew (Matt 2:13–23). Soon after the visit by the Magi, who had learned that King Herod intended to kill the infants of that area, an angel appeared to Joseph in a dream and told him to flee to Egypt with Mary and the young child Jesus. They fled to Egypt to hide within people who looked like them. If they were white, they would have stuck out like a sore thumb.

- In Acts 21:37-39;

  "And as Paul was to be led into the castle, he said unto the chief captain, May I speak unto thee? Who said, Canst thou speak Greek? Art

not thou that Egyptian, which before these days made an uproar, and led out into the wilderness four thousand men that were murderers? But Paul said, I am a man which am a Jew of Tarsus, a city in Cilicia, a citizen of no mean city: and, I beseech thee, suffer me to speak unto the people."

The Roman official mistook Paul to be Egyptian because of his black color.

- In Exodus 4:6-7;

"And the Lord said furthermore unto him, Put now thine hand into

thy bosom. And he put his hand into his bosom: and when he took it

out, behold, his hand was leprous (white) as snow. And he said, Put thine hand into thy bosom again. And he put his hand into his bosom again; and plucked it out of his bosom, and, behold, it was turned again as his other flesh."

If Moses had been white turning his hand white would have no shock effect like it did. It means he must have been black.

These are some of the evidences that Hebrew Israelites were and are a black people. We also have the Egyptian president confirming the Hebrew Israelites being black.

In our search for the true Hebrew Israelites we have established a case for the connection between the disappearance of the Jews and the appearance of the Bantus.

- ❖ We have seen the Jews disappearing into Africa and the Bantus appearing in Africa at about the same time in History.
- ❖ We have followed the written history of the Israelites in the bible and history of their enemies all the way to Africa where they disappeared, only to have the emergence of the Bantus, without prior historical records and thereafter only folklore.
- ❖ We have established that the Jews were running away as they came into Africa; and we have also seen the Bantus took on the relay baton and kept on running all over Africa.
- ❖ We have seen the color of the original Hebrew Israelites being black; same as the Bantus.
- ❖ We have established that the language of the Jews disappeared with them in Africa; we also see the Bantus who are the same people all over Africa and the world, yet their languages

are different, unless keenly examined and hidden similarities become apparent.

What now needs to be established is the fulfilment of scripture. We read in,

Deuteronomy 28:68;

"And the Lord shall bring thee into Egypt again with ships, by the way whereof I spake unto thee, thou shalt see it no more again: and there ye shall be sold unto your enemies for bondmen and bondwomen, and no man shall buy you."

This passage describes the Afro or African Americans perfectly. After escaping to Africa, the Jews, established the Kingdom of Juda in West Africa. This looks like it was a tactical error for it advertised their where about to their enemies. The Africans and Arabs captured and sold them to the Europeans who shipped them to the Americas as slaves. They were taken to Egypt again, in ships! in Deuteronomy 5:6 we know Egypt also refers to House of Bondage, and their destination to the Americas and elsewhere was a House of Bondage. As per the scriptures they escaped Canaan to Africa via Mt. Sinai where God had given them the Law and they have not gone back, they were transported in ships, and sold as slaves to their enemies; read Romans, in the Americas and nobody redeemed them – 'buy you'. No other people faced this kind of slavery with it's horrible mal-treatments that are beyond human understanding. Any horrible treatment imaginable, it happened to them. All Bantus faced terrible hardships and torture, like those of Congo; in the 23 years (1885-1908) Leopold II ruled the Congo he massacred over 10 million Bantus. He had their hands and genitals cut off, flogging them to death, starving them into forced labor, holding children ransom and burning villages. The Bantus (African Americans and others) in the Americas faced the blunt of it. The Bantus fulfil the prophesy of Deuteronomy 28 as communities in diaspora. These people are the Hebrew Israelites of old who became the Bantus and are known by a myriad of names, and they are black! One of the main names given to them is Negro which in Spanish means Black. When the Spanish became involved in the slave trade, they used the word Negro to describe Africans. Negro is an adjective which means black people in Portuguese and Spanish. The other name used is African- or Afro-, these are prefixes denoting the origin to be Africa. This is where we get African Americans and Afro-Caribbeans and Afro-Latin Americans. All these groups share one heritage. They are Bantu. The name Bantu is common among Bantu speakers in a variety of versions. A few of them are Watu, Antu, Abantu, Adu, Abandu etc.

It is now clear that the Hebrew Israelites are dispersed throughout the world as we read in,

Deuteronomy 4:25-28;

"when thou shalt beget children, and children's children, and ye shall have remained long in the land, and shall corrupt yourselves, and make a graven image, or the likeness of anything, and shall do evil in the sight of the Lord thy God, to provoke him to anger:

I call heaven and earth to witness against you this day, that ye shall soon utterly perish from off the land whereunto ye go over Jordan to possess it; ye shall not prolong your days upon it, but shall utterly be destroyed.

And the Lord shall scatter you among the nations, and ye shall be left few in number among the heathen, whither the Lord shall lead you.

And there ye shall serve gods, the work of men's hands, wood and stone, which neither see, nor hear, nor eat, nor smell".

If then, the children of Israel are not in Israel; who is?

There is no doubt the children of Israel are the black people dispersed all over the earth, known as Bantus, Negroes and others. They mostly do not know their heritage.

Chapter 8

AUDACITY

In this chapter we will establish the children of Israel were routed out of Israel completely by 135 C.E and they have not returned. A conspiracy was hatched to settle the children of Japheth in Israel, fulfilling the prophesy of Noah, thereby further blurring the memory of the real children of Israel as prophesied in Psalm 83. Pulling off this heist would put to naught the search for the children of Israel. After all they were repatriated back home in 1948!

The Biggest Secret in The World

Israel is a modern country among the nations, it boasts a robust economy with some of the highest per capita income. The nation of Israel was re-established by the United Nations in 1948. Prior to that the Northern Kingdom was taken into captivity by the Assyrians in 722 B.C.E. and they never returned. Israel as a nation ceased to exist around 70 C.E. and 135 C.E. when the Romans routed the Jews and dismantled Jerusalem killing many. It was described "as if they were demented", they killed the Jews until the dead formed heaps they had to climb over to kill more. Like one

Hebrew Israelite said, "they did us BAD". The Jews escaped, were killed or enslaved. By the end of the Roman campaign Israel was no more.

This mayhem was visited on Judea in 70 C.E. and 135 C.E., these events were already prophesied in Deuteronomy 4:28-25 and 28:68. By the time of the Messiah, it was a forgone conclusion. He told those in Judea to be ready to flee into the Mountains, cause of the impending doom. By this time Samaria, (the 10 Northern Tribes of Israel), was already dispersed through the Assyrian captivity, they never returned.

That is why they are known as the 10 lost tribes of Israel. By the coming of the Messiah, only three tribes were in Judea whose capital was Jerusalem. These are Judah and Benjamin and Levi. Please note the term Jew referred only to Judah, it came later to include the Benjaminite's and the Levite's who were co-located with them. Much later the term Jew, sometimes meant all Israelites. In the new Testament, you will note the Messiah commissioning his Disciples to go preach to the Nations. The Nations He was referring to, were the 10 tribes that were already in diaspora. Remember He said in, Matthew 15:24;

"I am not sent but unto the lost sheep of the house of

Israel".

In other scriptures referring to neither Jew nor Greek was calling upon the Jews in Judea and the Greeks meant the Israelites in diaspora. The term Greek or Gentile often referred to Israelites who were not practicing the law or forbidden to declare their identity.

The question now is, when Israel was recreated in 1948 by the United Nations, who settled there? One thing we do know, the people settled there call themselves Jews. The Ashkenazi Jews and the Sephardi Jews. These Jews never call themselves Hebrew Israelites! So, which tribe do they belong? Of the 12 tribes of Israel none were called Ashkenazi or Sephardi. If there is one thing we have learned in this journey, we can trace most people backwards to Noah's Sons. That's where we start.

In Genesis 10:1-5;

*"Now these are the generations of the sons of Noah, Shem, Ham, and Japheth: and unto them were sons born after the flood. The sons of Japheth; Gomer, and Magog, and Madai, and Javan, and Tubal, and Meshech, and Tiras. And the sons of Gomer; **Ashkenaz,** and Riphath, and Togarmah. And the sons of Javan; Elishah, and Tarshish, Kittim, and Dodanim. By these were the isles of the Gentiles divided in their lands; everyone after his*

tongue, after their families, in their nations".

We have quickly established that the Ashkenazi were of the blood line of Japheth. They are not of the bloodline of Shem of which the Hebrew Israelites belong. They are from Eastern Europe between the Caucus Mountains and the Black sea. This area was called Khazaria and the people, Khazars. How they come to be in Palestine and Jews is another story.

The other group of Jews in Israel are the Sephardic's. The actual Jews also referred to as the "Jews of Spain" became a community in the Iberian Peninsula spreading through-out Spain and Portugal by around 1000 C.E. They were Black and were expelled from Spain in 1492 by King Ferdinand and Queen Isabella. These Jews migrated to Africa. The Caucasian Sephardic Jews who migrated to Israel in 1948 were not Hebrew Israelites but possible converts. The two groups of Jews in Israel do not also conform to the prophesy, *"thou shalt see it no more again"*. If they managed to return on their own, it means they do not fulfill scripture and therefore cannot be true Hebrew Israelites, unless somebody wants to doubt the Most High.

The essence of this book is not to dwell on who is not or where they came from, their fate is with the Most

High, but to awaken the children of Israel whose identity has been stolen. It will suffice to know the current occupants of the land of Israel are not the true inheritors of the promise. THEY ARE NOT HEBREW ISRAELITES. They are impostors. It's with pity and awe we perceive their future. They shall be held accountable for their transgressions. If the Most High could chastise His beloved children like He did us by turning His back on us all these years, then how much more will He bring to account those that have subjugated His children and parted His land. Revelation 2:9 and 3:9 makes it clear the LORD knew of their actions, He calls them *"the synagogue of Satan"* and He will make them worship at our feet.

Majority of the children of Israel do not know their true identity. They think, those in Israel are the real Israelites. After they were routed out and dispersed, those that survived were forbidden to return to their homeland. Israel was even given a new name, *"Syria Palestina"*. From 135 C.E. to 1948, a period of 1813 years, there was no Israel. How then could we not forget? Also take note our ancestors were not broadcasting our where about for fear of being found and subjugated. Or so we thought! It is apparent our enemies knew all along who we were and where we were. That's why they were confident in their actions against us, for they knew of our relationship with our GOD. They are the ones who were the conquerors, they lied about our history, they confiscated our written knowledge. They own our history. They even left out whole books from our history, the bible. The books they conveniently omitted were those that would have given us clues of who we are. They forced us to take other identities and culture. But like in the times of the Exodus we will go back home, with much substance! All these years they have persecuted and exacted free labor from Gods people and waxed strong and wealthy on the back of His children, they will pay and pay in full they shall. This crime was visited on the children of Israel by the children Japheth and those of Ham and the other Shemetic Hebrews - children of Abraham that were not Jacobs seed, turned their backs on us. One thing to take note of; in their efforts to blot us out of existence, they took our identity, customs, history and all, there-by incubating for us our history. The Most High made our enemies conserve the records that would eventually undo their conspiracy. It's ironic when thieves steal and later, convince themselves of the legitimacy of ownership. How dumb!

Where are the children of Israel now? The safest answer is everywhere. The LORD in Deuteronomy 28:25 *"caused them to be removed into all the Kingdoms of the earth"*. The Jews left Israel as Hebrew Israelites and became Bantus in Africa, then they were referred to as Negros in Africa and other places where they underwent forced migration. They were also referred to as Africans. All these names are by-words, especially African. Let all and sundry know, we the Bantus, "ARE NOT AFRICANS" or any other designation like "NEGROES". "WE ARE HEBREW ISRAELITES!"

All these efforts I see of blessing the Israelites pursuant to Genesis 12:3 are fruitless. Those in Israel are the children of Japheth. Your gift will be better utilized blessing your local Black Hebrew Israelite. You can't miss them, they are everywhere. Not to mention that reparations are in order, and will be forcefully exacted (Rev 2:26, Acts 3:20, Job 20:4, Isa 14:1, Isa 60:10, 2 Esdras 9). To date the administration in Israel denies the true Israelites entry into their homeland. These are the same people who owned the ships that carried Hebrew Israelites to slavery to the Americas, they owned the auction blocks, and they owned the plantations. They are still exacting a heavy burden on them through industry and commerce. They own the media houses, they own the printing presses and they even own our history, the bible. They have stolen and corrupted our identity, they control our education, entertainment and living. They snicker at us, but as sure as the sun rises from the East, they will pay, their time is almost up. The end is near. Let all Israel know of the good news, then the end will come. Matthew 24:14;

"And this gospel of the kingdom shall be preached in all the world for a witness unto all nations; and then shall the end come."

The real children of Israel are still in diaspora. They are all over the world. They are called by a myriad of names, mainly Bantus, Negroes, E.T.C. The biggest concentrations are in Africa, South America, North America and the Islands, Europe and Middle East. Those that were allowed back by the authorities in Israel, face hardships and discrimination. It goes without saying that, trying to relocate to Israel is unproductive and against scripture. When the Israelites were removed from their homeland, the LORD told them "they shall see it no more". Wherever you are, make the best of it and wait for the gathering of the Lord as prophesied.

Chapter 9

GENEALOGY

We have journeyed together this far in search of the truth relating to the heritage of the Bantu people. One must ask, why is all this necessary? One of the answers is pride of ancestry, the other is to answer the old age question – why Am I here? What is my true Nationality? The answer to the second, of course has implications of responsibilities and expectations. Let's play with ....

Science

When the children of Israel come into the knowledge of their ancestry, some of the questions asked is:

How do I know for sure I'm a Hebrew Israelite?

I'm Black, been called African, been called a Bantu, been called a Negro or other names.

I know for sure I'm not Egyptian, Canaanite, Ethiopian or Libyan.

This only tells me I'm not Hamitic, therefore not African!

So, if one is black and not African, what are they?

To start answering this question, we look in the bible. The findings of the bible are further reinforced with modern science. In the book of Genesis and Numbers we get a lot of begats. From Genesis 4 we get the genealogy of the family of Cain and in Genesis 5 the family of Adam his father. The bible clearly records who begat who and how many years they lived. One thing to note is the family tree which is from father to son. In the lineage of Adam, Lamech begat Noah. During the great flood, all the people of earth were killed except Noah and his family. From Noah's three sons, we have all the people of earth. In Genesis 10 the begats continue. The family of each of Noah's sons is carefully recorded. The family tree, who they became and where they settled is all there. One thing to note is the continuation of father to son lineage. Although, women are mentioned, it's the father son lineage that is followed. Let no one confuse you; you have only one lineage through your father, his father, his father and so on to Noah and beyond. Some naysayers will try to convince you that you are what your parents are, their parents, their parents etcetera, this is only in blood but not genes.

In the lineage of Shem, we see the same careful tracking of the family tree all the way to Abraham. He was the first Hebrew, and all his descendants are Hebrews. This includes Ismael and Isaac, plus the other children of his wife Keturah and all their progeny. In the lineage of Isaac, we again see the careful recording of the children of Jacob, his second born, who inherited the firstborn's blessings. The ancestry of Jacob's children, who are known as the 12 tribes of Israel is also meticulously recorded. Until after the exodus the children of Israel could trace their ancestry, all the way to Adam. When the Israelites returned home to Canaan after the exodus from Egypt, they encountered several upheavals of war and forced migration that tore the very fabric of their Nation-hood. Yet, we can see the lineage of the children of Israel being recorded even during these upheavals. The lineage of Judah to Yeshua who was born during the Roman occupation is recorded. These calamities peaked around 135 C.E. when they were routed out of Israel by the Romans and forbidden to return. Their Nation was even renamed 'Syria Palestina'. From this dispersal, they were in diaspora and after almost two thousand years away from home and dispersed all over the earth, the careful recording of their history and ancestry was no more. Their history and stock of knowledge was stolen. Even the bible, which is a record of God and His relationship with His children is in the hands of the Gentiles.

How then can we ascertain who they are?

This is where science and history converge. We saw clearly that God established the ancestry of the people from father to son. Any person can only trace their ancestry through Y-DNA Haplo group mapping. God knew and established this truth before the advent of modern science. In the previous chapters we established that the Hebrew Israelites are a black people, they look like the Africans, but they are not Africans. By far they do not know who they are. We also established that they can be found all over the earth going by many names. The search is narrowed further, because the Hamites are known. These are the Egyptians, Canaanites, Libyans and Ethiopians. If you are black, and you know you are not a Hamite, then there is a high chance you are a Hebrew Israelite. This analogy is for men. For women, the proof is with your father. This line of reasoning is only good if the father-son ancestry has remained true. When a child is born it's, ancestry follows the fathers side. Example; if a Hebrew Israelite woman has a child with a white or African man, that child is not a Hebrew Israelite. This complicates ancestry mapping, but there is a solution. If one knows in their heart they are Hebrew Israelite, then most likely they are. If they want to know for sure, then they will have to undergo DNA testing. The results will establish their Y-DNA Haplogroup. Women who wish to determine their direct paternal DNA ancestry, can ask their father or close male relative to take a test for them.

The Africans are predominantly E-M215 also known as E1b1b, with two branches, the E-M35 and E-M281 subclades.

The E-M35 has two branches, haplogroup E-V68 and E-Z827, which are found in North Africa and the Horn of Africa respectfully.

E-M281 is found mainly in Ethiopia.

The analogy continues further; if you are black and not African, then the chances of you being Hebrew Israelite are even higher. From here, we use elimination and bible record, history and prophesy. In the bible, it is prophesied the curses that would befall the children of Israel if they did not keep their covenant with their God. Of note is Deuteronomy 28 where the final punishment is declared to be slavery in a far-off land where they would be taken in ships. The only people who are black; are from or passed through Africa; are not Hamites;

taken to slavery in ships; have not been redeemed; are the so called "Africans" or "Negroes" taken to the Americas during the infamous Trans-Atlantic slave trade. By reverse tracking, we can ascertain that the so called African Americans and Afro-Latin Americans are the bona-fide children of Israel. They are black and not African. They were rounded up by the Africans and Arabs who sold them to the European slave traders. The Africans knew they were not selling fellow Africans but sojourners from without. They were in Africa where they ended up after being routed out by their enemies in Mesopotamia. We established earlier how the Jews escaped into Africa and disappeared into the vast continent. Unbeknown to them, their enemies were not far off. These are the Hebrew Israelites who escaped to Africa only for some to be driven further as slaves into the Americas and elsewhere. These people were baptized the name Bantus or Negroes. They are dispersed all over the world, but mostly found in Africa South of the Sahara. All those in Africa were colonized; read slavery. We read in Zephaniah 3:10;

"From beyond the rivers of Ethiopia my suppliants, even the daughter of my dispersed, shall bring mine offering."

Daughter means Israel.

From the Holy land, beyond the rivers of Ethiopia would be the Bantu territory of Sub-Saharan Africa. The countries bordering Ethiopia to the South are Kenya, Uganda, East Africa, Central Africa and Southern Africa. These countries have large Bantu populations, unlike those in the North, which are predominantly Hamitic. The LORD is telling us, His children are there. The term 'My dispersed' is the LORD'S reference to the Jews who were routed out by the Romans in 70 – 135 C.E.

By elimination, we have black people who are not Africans. They are mainly in Africa. They are also found all over the world in conformity with scripture, and some of them are in America in fulfillment to Deuteronomy 28 curses. They must be the Hebrew Israelites. They are the Hebrew Israelites, and their Y-DNA Haplogroup is predominantly E-V38 with two basal branches, E-M329 (formerly E1b1c) and E-M2 (formerly E1b1a).

The E-M329 subscale is today almost exclusively found in Ethiopia. E-M2 is the predominant subscale in Western Africa, Central Africa, Southern Africa, Eastern Africa, the Americas and all Bantus or Negroes.

When I became convicted of the knowledge of this

truth I had no doubt of my heritage. I knew in my heart of hearts that I was a Hebrew Israelite. The knowledge had an astounding effect on my life. I was so convinced that even my outlook on many things changed. The pain I felt for my ancestors was almost physical and I could really feel their pain and their despair. Many a time I wept for my people. The bible took on a new meaning for my life and I know I will never be the same again. I had previously been contented to be a servant in heaven, like all gentiles that make it. I knew it was better than hell, but was honest in knowing that non-Israelites in heaven will be servants to the children of God. Now I know, I'm Israelite and long for heaven. I know I will rule with my God. This is the promise of God to His children, the Hebrew Israelites. It's our heritage. It is after sharing these profound truths with my wife Esther and our children Derrick and Julian, that they encouraged me to write this book. I never thought myself as the writing type, but this knowledge has a power of its own. It cannot be contained. It must get out there. What you do with it is up to you.

To proceed writing this book, I had to proof the theory of the DNA mapping. I had to show those in doubt a way to ascertain their ancestry. I procured a test kit and omitted my background. The results as shown indicate that my nearest relatives are the African Americans. That statement caught me completely off guard.

Your Predicted Haplogroup is E-M2

| THOMAS G| | THOMAS G| | Search

Haplogroup E is an African lineage. It is currently believed that this haplogroup dispersed south from northern Africa with the Bantu agricultural expansion. E is also the most common lineage among African Americans. It is a diverse haplogroup with many branches and is found distributed throughout Africa today. It is also found at a very low frequency in North Africa and the Middle East.

You must be able to discern the wiles of these people. Notice they mention African and Bantu in the same breath. They want you to think you are African which is not true, since E-M2 is not African but Hebrew Israelite which is Semitic. They sugar-coat the information with "Bantu agricultural expansion" instead of plainly saying you are Bantu. They say this Haplogroup is African that dispersed with the Bantu expansion. So, if they are African moving along with the Bantus, who are the Bantus? Where did they come from? Also, we note the low frequency of this group in North Africa and the Middle East the explanation is simple. In North Africa you will find the African Hamites and in the Middle East you will find the Hamitic Canaanites. All these are E-M215. The Israelites who are E-M2 would be found in the Middle East, but we know they were routed out by the Romans to a man as of 135 C.E., and they became the Bantus. They did not stop in North Africa for their enemies were after them, they kept moving deeper into Africa. We also note the E-M329 in Ethiopia. These are the Israelites who moved out of the Northern Kingdom and disappeared before the Assyrian conquest, and possibly the family of Solomon. Those in Israel are not Hebrew Israelites.

It is possible to pursue these lines if one is interested but be wary of their snares. The owners of these tools and information are not your friends. I'm not in any way advocating any course of action, other than, for those affected to study the bible for yourself, with renewed interest in those characters for they are your relatives. In Matthew 13:24 we read the parable of the wheat and tares. The weeds (Gentiles), will grow with us. At the appointed time, the harvesters (Angels) will uproot them to be burned, and the wheat (His children) will be taken to His barn (heaven). The harvesters will differentiate the Children of God from the impostors. The LORD knew about these impostor's way before. Science has given us the tools to know if we are the wheat. And those that are not, but are willing to sojourn with us, that's another story.

Wake up oh Israel!

The great slumber that afflicts the children of Israel will soon come to an end.

Why is this important?

Those that hold your history know the outcome of your waking up. Jesus told the Disciples In,

Mathew 24:14;

"And this gospel of the kingdom shall be preached in all the world for a witness unto all nations; and then shall the end come."

The only people who will preach this gospel, in truth, is the children of Israel. Who can understand scripture? We read in, Isaiah 28:9-11;

"Whom shall he teach knowledge? and whom shall he make to understand doctrine? them that are weaned from the milk, and drawn from the breasts. For precept must be upon precept, precept upon precept; line upon line, line upon line; here a little, and there a little: For with stammering lips and another tongue will he speak to this people."

All the tongues we speak are foreign to us. We can never

be perfect. That's why we have accents in which ever language we speak.

Who can understand scripture?

Those that, follow the commandments and, are prophets of Israel,

- Psalms 111:10;

  "The fear of the Lord is the beginning of wisdom: a good understanding have all they that do his commandments: his praise endureth for ever."

- Amos 3:7;

  "Surely the Lord God will do nothing, but he revealeth his secret unto his servants the prophets."

- Ezekiel 38:17;

  "Thus saith the Lord God; Art thou he of whom I have spoken in old time by my servants the prophets of Israel, which prophesied in those days many years that I would bring thee against them?"

Those who wake up must preach to those in slumber. They must preach to the nations (children of Israel), because they must be privy to these truths, and they are dispersed all over the world.

The LORD also lets us know the recipe,

In 2 Chronicles 7:14;

"If my people, which are called by my name, shall humble themselves, and pray, and seek my face, and turn from their wicked ways; then will I hear from heaven, and will forgive their sin, and will heal their land."

This scenario is prayed out in the prayer of Jehoshaphat of 2 Chronicles 20. When all Israel comes to the LORD in corporate prayer He hears and acts on it. That is why even the contract Israel entered with the LORD in Deuteronomy 24, the LORD accepted it and held all of them accountable, because they all agreed. In view of this, if all Israel came into corporate prayer, repented and cried out to the LORD, then He would hear and the end we so eagerly await would come. This would usher a new dispensation where the Israelite is the ruler and the gentiles the servants. I'm reminded of one Kenyan post-independence patriotic song "previously we were no. 4, "but now it's about-turn and we are no. 1". Recently two African presidents acted reminiscent to 2 Chronicles 20. The Kenyan and Zambian presidents rallied their countrymen to corporate prayer. The emotions especially of the Zambian meeting, though in 1993 are still palpable to this day. I'm sure the outcomes of these meetings touched the Most High as implied in 2 chronicles 7:14 and were answered. Kenya and Zambia have large Bantu populations and whether they know it or not, they are Israelites. The world was made for our sake, the rest are nothing. We read in,

2 Esdras 6:54-59;

"And after these, Adam also, whom thou madest lord of all thy creatures: of him come we all, and the people also whom thou hast chosen. All this have I spoken before thee, O Lord, because thou madest the world for our sakes. As for the other people, which also come of Adam, thou hast said that they are nothing, but be like unto spittle: and hast likened the abundance of them unto a drop that falleth from a vessel. And now, O Lord, behold, these heathen, which have ever been reputed as nothing, have begun to be lords over us, and to devour us. But we thy people, whom thou hast called thy firstborn, thy only begotten, and thy fervent lover, are given into their hands. If the world now be made for our sakes, why do we not possess an inheritance with the world? how long shall this endure?"

We get the same confirmation in,

Isaiah 40:15-17;

"Behold, the nations are as a drop of a bucket, and are

counted as the small dust of the balance: behold, he taketh up the isles as a very little thing. And Lebanon is not sufficient to burn, nor the beasts thereof sufficient for a burnt offering. All nations before him are as nothing; and they are counted to him less than nothing, and vanity".

So, what happens to the gentiles?

One of the reasons they don't want the children of Israel to wake up is tied to the outcome of the awakening. The scriptures do not promise a rosy ending, especially for those who subjugated His children (Psalms 83:2-8). They that enslaved them, forced them to migrate or exacted forced labor, will pay a heavy price. They and their descendants. The children of Israel are in subjugation in payment of their ancestor's deeds. It follows then, the children of our enemies will pay. In full. Sudden like. The Lord chastises us as we err, but for the heathen, it will be once, in full. Just like a father who loves his child punishes him, we should appreciate our Fathers chastisement, for it is a measure of His love, to save us from eternal damnation. The slain of the LORD shall be many as we read in, Isaiah 66:14-16;

"And when ye see this, your heart shall rejoice, and your bones shall flourish like an herb: and the hand of the

Lord shall be known toward his servants, and his indignation toward his enemies.

For, behold, the Lord will come with fire, and with his chariots like a whirlwind, to render his anger with fury, and his rebuke with flames of fire.

For by fire and by his sword will the Lord plead with all flesh: and the slain of the Lord shall be many."

Isaiah 63:1-4;

"Who is this that cometh from Edom, with dyed garments from Bozrah? this that is glorious in his apparel, travelling in the greatness of his strength? I that speak in righteousness, mighty to save. Wherefore art thou red in thine apparel, and thy garments like him that treadeth in the winefat? I have trodden the winepress alone; and of the people there was none with me: for I will tread them in mine anger, and trample them in my fury; and their blood shall be sprinkled upon my garments, and I will stain all my raiment. For the day of vengeance is in mine heart, and the year of my redeemed is come."

The day of the LORD is coming; Christ will kill many Edomites and Ishmaelites as indicated in Psalms 83:6.

We conclude that there are scientific ways to establish your ancestry. This is for your peace of mind and pride of heritage. On the day of the LORD, His angels will gather His elect – the children of Israel who have followed His commandments (Mathew 13:29-30, Isaiah 45:4, Ezekiel 20:33-39), the rebels will not enter His gathering. The gentiles that are found worthy will not be abandoned but will serve in the Kingdom of our God as servants and maids (Zechariah 8:23, Isaiah 61:5-7, Isaiah 14:1-2). The unfortunate thing is, those that are in the know are too proud to accept this coming status. They are ready to enjoy their heaven in the present dispensation and lead their compatriots to eternal condemnation.

Chapter 10

FREEDOM

So far, we have established who the real Israelites are. The question that needs an answer is, when will the slavery we find ourselves in, end. All Israelites without exception are in slavery now, whether they know it or not! Even the very rich of our people, are just rich slaves.

Even those with 'sovereign' countries are still slaves of their masters, for their effort is to enrich them.

This slavery we can't get ourselves out off.

This slavery is a state of mind as it is physical.

It's also called neo-colonialism

Awakening

I'm reminded of the Reggae music of the 1980's, more so the one of Bob Marley; Redemption song! The lyrics talk about slavery of the mind. The colonial powers would have you believe that their former colonies of slaves had been freed. But were they? What Bob was advocating was for the 'former' slaves to realize they were still in slavery. The slavery of the mind. Part of slavery was to indoctrinate the slaves in self-hate and aspire to be like the master. Who has not seen the Bantus parting their hair or straightening and wearing imitations, lightening their skins etcetera. This indoctrination was forcibly instilled to the extent the victims lost their former identity. This phenomenon was world-wide. It did not matter what the masters called themselves or their subjects. They had all confederated to subjugate the children of Israel. This song was a veiled wake-up call for the children of Israel World-wide, to realize their state of slavery; **"emancipate yourself from mental slavery, none but ourselves can free our mind, ooh they say it's just a part of it, we have to fulfill the book, won't you help me sing, this song of freedom."**

It means free yourself from mental slavery; the book is the bible, which the aggressors used as a guide to the curses that were to befall the children of Israel as per Deuteronomy 28, but they used the curse of Canaan as the excuse for enslaving us, thereby making us believe erroneously we were Africans as per Genesis 9:25-27;

Then he said:

"Cursed be Canaan; A servant of servants
He shall be to his brethren."

And he said:

"Blessed be the Lord, The God of Shem, And may

Canaan be his servant. May God enlarge Japheth, And may he dwell in the tents of Shem; And may Canaan be his servant."

They had robbed the children of Israel their Identity, religion, culture, wealth and stock of knowledge. They had even stolen their God and Savior. They installed a white man named Cesare Borgia as the face of Jesus although we know Jesus was black as were all Israelites. They also disregarded,

Exodus 20:4;

"Thou shalt not make unto thee any graven image, or any likeness of anything that is in heaven above, or that is in the earth beneath, or that is in the water under the earth."

They even translated the name of the Savior from Yeshua to Jesus. Why was it necessary to change His name and likeness? In normal translations, names are usually not translated, unless it can't be spelt in the new language, but not so with Yeshua. His name need not have been translated into the English Jesus. If your name is Peter does it become Pierre if you visit France? Or if your name is Njoroge, doesn't it still remain Njoroge in America? Please note the letter J was created in the eighteenth century. They changed his name to hide his identity from the children of Israel.

We note in Revelation 1:14-15;

"His head and his hairs were white like wool, as white as snow; and his eyes were as a flame of fire; And his feet like unto fine brass, as if they burned in a furnace; and his voice as the sound of many waters."

A BLACK MAN'S DESCRIPTION!

The man now portrayed as Jesus is; Cesare Borgia, his father was Rodrigo Borgia also known as Pope Alexander VI. The Catholic Church gave consent for this man to use the image of his son (who was really Cesare Borgia) to be put up and portrayed as Jesus Christ in order to deceive the whole world! He is not the Messiah, the Son of God. Why would they hide? If you knew the truth, you might figure out you are the biblical Israelites. How will we gain this freedom?

The book of Amos chapter 9, details how the LORD will destroy His enemies on the day of the LORD. Even those of the house of Israel that are sinners will be destroyed, but a remnant will be saved.

In verse 9;

"For, lo, I will command, and I will sift the house of Israel among all nations, like as corn is sifted in a sieve,

yet shall not the least grain fall upon the earth."

In verse 14;

"And I will bring again the captivity of my people of Israel, and they shall build the waste cities, and inhabit them; and they shall plant vineyards, and drink the wine thereof; they shall also make gardens, and eat the fruit of them."

This is the promise that God has for Israel, unimaginable blessings. It is also the opposite or remedy for the curses of Deuteronomy 28.

In verse 12;

"That they may possess the remnant of Edom, and of all the heathen, which are called by my name, saith the Lord that doeth this."

The LORD promises to bring together the children of Israel from wherever they are scattered. He shall make them possess the remnant of Edom and the heathen that are called by His name. The Edomites as a people allegedly integrated themselves with the Romans and are one and the same. This is a representation of all the other people that are not destroyed. They shall be possessions of the Israelites. The reference to, the remnant of Edom and the heathen called by His name, encompasses all non-Israelites that make it to heaven.

We read in Isaiah 11:15-16;

"And the Lord shall utterly destroy the tongue of the Egyptian sea; and with his mighty wind shall he shake his hand over the river, and shall smite it in the seven streams, and make men go over dry shod. And there shall be an highway for the remnant of his people, which shall be left, from Assyria; like as it was to Israel in the day that he came up out of the land of Egypt."

All these are metaphors of the LORD saying his children will come back home from all directions, and He shall get rid of all obstacles.

Isaiah 14:1;

"For the Lord will have mercy on Jacob, and will yet choose Israel, and set them in their own land: and the strangers shall be joined with them, and they shall cleave to the house of Jacob."

Amos 9:15;

"*And I will plant them upon their land, and they shall no more be pulled up out of their land which I have given them, saith the LORD thy God."*

Here again the LORD assures the former kingdoms of Judah and Israel will become one – Israel. During the exodus from Egypt, a multitude of other nationalities, who were slaves in Egypt, accompanied the children of

Israel, even this time sojourners will be welcome.

In Isaiah 11:11-12;

"And it shall come to pass in that day, that the Lord shall set his hand again the second time to recover the remnant of his people, which shall be left, from Assyria, and from Egypt, and from Pathros, and from Cush, and from Elam, and from Shinar, and from Hamath, and from the islands of the sea. And he shall set up an ensign for the nations, and shall assemble the outcasts of Israel, and gather together the dispersed of Judah from the four corners of the earth."

This is the salvation that is promised the children of Israel! The remnants are the ten tribes and the dispersed are three tribes. An ensign is a military or Nationality flag declaring sovereignty or the seat of power. Israel will be under one authority, of our God, YHWH. The rest of the world that make it to heaven will be the possession of the children of Israel. Those that are masters now will be servants and handmaids, so says the LORD in,

Isaiah 14:2;

"And the people shall take them, and bring them to their place: and the house of Israel shall possess them in the land of the Lord for servants and handmaids: and they

shall take them captives, whose captives they were; and they shall rule over their oppressors."

Even Jesus made it clear in Mathew 15:22-27;

"And, behold, a woman of Canaan came out of the same coasts, and cried unto him, saying, have mercy on me, O, thou son of David; my daughter is grievously vexed with a devil. But he answered her not a word. And his disciples came and besought him, saying, Send her away; for she crieth after us. But he answered and said, I am not sent but unto the lost sheep of the house of Israel. Then came she and worshipped him, saying, Lord, help me. But he answered and said, It is not meet to take the children's bread, and to cast it to dogs. And she said, Truth, Lord: yet the dogs eat of the crumbs which fall from their masters' table."

Jesus tells the African woman, He came for the purpose of uplifting the children of Israel, not wasting his time on everybody.

The Canaanite woman representing the heathens concurs that the Israelites are the coming masters and they, the heathens are like dogs (servants).

Verse 28;

"Then Jesus answered and said unto her, O woman, great is thy faith: be it unto thee even as thou wilt. And

her daughter was made whole from that very hour."

This confirms that heathens that believe can be saved.

Featured along the Children of Israel, we find a lot of mention of the children of Esau or the Edomites. Esau the elder brother of Jacob is prophesied as the end of the current dispensation and Jacob is the beginning of the kingdom of heaven.

2 Esdras 6:9;

"For Esau is the end of the world, and Iacob is the beginning of it that followeth."

The LORD also said in, Romans 9:13;

"As it is written, Jacob have I loved, but Esau have I hated."

This cause of the violence the children of Esau visited on the children of Israel during their trouble. Of note is during the destruction of Jerusalem in 70 C.E., the Israelites that managed to escape the slaughter, were prevented from escaping by the Edomites that were positioned at the cross roads, in cahoots with the Romans.

It's written in Malachi 1:2-4;

"I have loved you, saith the Lord. Yet ye say, wherein hast thou loved us? Was not Esau Jacob's brother? saith the Lord: yet I loved Jacob, And I hated Esau, and laid *his mountains and his heritage waste for the dragons of the wilderness. Whereas Edom saith, We are impoverished, but we will return and build the desolate places; thus saith the Lord of hosts, They shall build, but I will throw down; and they shall call them, The border of wickedness, and, The people against whom the Lord hath indignation forever."*

So where are the Edomites?

They were absolved by the children of Japheth, the Romans, and through them the children of Japheth were poisoned.

The book of Jasher chapter 9;

1. At that time in the fifth year after the children of Israel had passed over Jordan, after the children of Israel had rested from their war with the Canaanites, at that time great and severe battles arose between Edom and the children of Chittim, and the children of Chittim fought against Edom.

2. And Abianus king of Chittim went forth in that year, that is in the thirty-first year of his reign, and a great force with him of the mighty men of the children of Chittim, and he went to Seir to fight against the children of Esau.

3. And Hadad the king of Edom heard of his report, and

he went forth to meet him with a heavy people and strong force, and engaged in battle with him in the field of Edom.

4. And the hand of Chittim prevailed over the children of Esau, and the children of Chittim slew of the children of Esau, two and twenty thousand men, and all the children of Esau fled from before them.

5. And the children of Chittim pursued them and they reached Hadad king of Edom, who was running before them and they caught him alive, and brought him to Abianus king of Chittim.

6. And Abianus ordered him to be slain, and Hadad king of Edom died in the forty-eighth year of his reign.

7. And the children of Chittim continued their pursuit of Edom, and they smote them with a great slaughter and Edom became subject to the children of Chittim.

8. And the children of Chittim ruled over Edom, and Edom became under the hand of the children of Chittim and became one kingdom from that day.

Chittim today;

History informs us that "Edom was conquered by Albianus, King of Chittim, and Edom became under the children of Chittim from that day;" and this is the reason the Prophet Isaiah speaks, in his 23rd chapter, connectively of Edom and Chittim as one and the same place and people. Chittim was representative of the European coasts of the Mediterranean Sea. These includes the Romans, who were the conquerors of Edom. The Assyrian Empire encompassed the Chaldea whose capital was Babylon, first established by Nimrod. This became the Roman Empire. The Romans peopled the West, Italy, Rome, France, England and America. Christianity became the established religion, under Constantine hence Babylon, Rome, Edom, and Christianity are synonymous.

We also know all Protestants first separated themselves from the Roman Catholics church at the Reformation. So, by this we see Protestants are of the seed of Rome, and Rome is of the seed of Chittim. Rome and Edom are one. Psalm 137:7-9;

"Remember, O Lord, the children of Edom in the day of Jerusalem; who said, Rase it, rase it, even to the foundation thereof. O daughter of Babylon, who art to be destroyed; happy shall he be, that rewardeth thee as thou hast served us. Happy shall he be, that taketh and dasheth thy little ones against the stones."

The Roman-Edom integration poisoned Japheth and they are headed for destruction.

Who are the Romans-Edomites now?

There are many scriptures and historical data on who they are. They integrated themselves together and became one, and thereafter seeded Japheth or Europeans. The most telling scripture is,

Deuteronomy 28: 68,

*"And the Lord shall bring thee into Egypt again with ships, by the way whereof I spake unto thee, Thou shalt see it no more again: and there ye shall be **sold unto your enemies** for bondmen and bondwomen, and no man shall buy you."*

Why is The Lord telling us the obvious? Of course, the buyers of the slaves were not friends! Why mention it? The answer is, The Lord is giving us a clue. Psalms 83 lists some of the enemies and these are relatives or neighbors of the Israelites. Of note is the Edomites. They integrated themselves with the Romans. In view of this, the enemies of Israel the LORD is telling us is the Romans-Edomite. They routed the Jews from their homeland then they bought the Jews as slaves in the Americas. The Roman-Edomites are also the Europeans that settled the Americas. They and the Ishmaelites are first on God's hit list.

In this chapter we have established that the curses of

Deuteronomy 28 that befell the children of Israel are still in force. All Israel without exception is in slavery. You might argue, but we have countries ruled by Israelites! That's true, but what percentage is financially free? Just as it happened in Egypt so is now.

We note in,

Exodus1:7-10;

"And the children of Israel were fruitful, and increased abundantly, and multiplied, and waxed exceeding mighty; and the land was filled with them. Now there arose up a new king over Egypt, which knew not Joseph. And he said unto his people, Behold, the people of the children of Israel are more and mightier than we: Come on, let us deal wisely with them; lest they multiply, and it come to pass, that, when there falleth out any war, they join also unto our enemies, and fight against us, and so get them up out of the land."

How did they deal with us wisely?

They employed our people to be officers, and if the quarters were not filled, the task masters punished the officers. This is illustrated in,

Exodus 5:14;

"And the officers of the children of Israel, which Pharaoh's taskmasters had set over them, were beaten,

and demanded, Wherefore have ye not fulfilled your task in making brick both yesterday and today, as heretofore?"

All Israel is in slavery. We are being punished for our sins, and we should be delighted for that, because it's out of love. We read in,

Proverbs 3:11-12;

"My son, do not despise the chastening of the Lord, Nor detest His correction; for whom the Lord loves He corrects, Just as a father the son in whom he delights."

Those sovereign countries have officers (presidents) over us. If we do not produce (balance of payments) our officers are punished, and they oppress us more - read taxes, concessions for aid, lopsided trade agreements E.T.C.

We have also established, this slavery we cannot get ourselves out off. Only our LORD GOD ALMIGHTY will free His children.

We have also established salvation is for the righteous children of Israel. The wicked will be destroyed with the heathen. The heathen that make it to heaven will be possessed by the children of Israel as servants and handmaids (Isaiah 14:2).

One thing to be wary of is religion. The relationship of religion and Edom, read Rome, read Roman Catholic, read Babylon (Babylon was Roman-Edomite center of operations to rule after they took over the former Assyrian Empire), especially mystery Babylon it's confusion and destruction. We read,

Revelation 17:5;

And upon her forehead was a name written, MYSTERY, BABYLON THE GREAT, THE MOTHER OF HARLOTS AND ABOMINATIONS OF THE EARTH.

Chapter 11

YOUR KINGDOM COME

As we close this narrative it's important to plan our next move.

We know that the kingdom of God is nigh.

We know salvation is a preserve of the Israelites-the chosen people of God.

The question now arises; now that I know my heritage, how do I book my spot in the coming dispensation- ***The Kingdom of Our GOD?***

Salvation

Those of the house of Israel that persevere will be saved. We have already established that, to the Israelite salvation is being in the kingdom of our God. There will be war. The Almighty God and His children will war against Babylon the great and other world rulers, resisting the kingdom of our God. He will establish His kingdom on earth, ruling with His children. Those of the gentiles that are found worthy will be incorporated into the new kingdom as servants and maid servants.

What is soon to follow.

We read in Romans 3:1-2;

"What advantage then hath the Jew (Israelite)? or what

profit is there of circumcision (covenant between God and Abraham)?

Much every way: chiefly, because that unto them were committed the oracles (laws) of God."

Daniel 12:1-2;

"And at that time shall Michael stand up, the great prince which standeth for the children of thy people: and there shall be a time of trouble, such as never was since there was a nation even to that same time: and at that time thy people shall be delivered, every one that shall be found written in the book. And many of them that sleep in the dust of the earth shall awake, some to everlasting life, and some to shame and everlasting contempt."

1 Chronicles 17:22;

"For thy people Israel didst thou make thine own people for ever; and thou, Lord, becamest their God."

Jeremiah 23:5-6;

"Behold, the days come, saith the Lord, that I will raise unto David a righteous Branch, and a King shall reign and prosper, and shall execute judgment and justice in the earth.

In his days Judah shall be saved, and Israel shall dwell safely: and this is his name whereby he shall be called,

THE LORD OUR RIGHTEOUSNESS."

Zechariah 8:13;

"And it shall come to pass, that as ye were a curse among the heathen, O house of Judah, and house of Israel; so will I save you, and ye shall be a blessing: fear not, but let your hands be strong."

Luke 1:68-74;

"Blessed be the Lord God of Israel; for he hath visited and redeemed his people, And hath raised up an horn (Jesus) of salvation for us in the house of his servant David; As he spake by the mouth of his holy prophets, which have been since the world began: that we should be saved from our enemies, and from the hand of all that hate us; to perform the mercy promised to our fathers, and to remember his holy covenant: the oath which he sware to our father Abraham, that he would grant unto us, that we being delivered out of the hand of our enemies might serve him without fear,"

The following letter was written by Paul to the dispersed Israelites of the Northern Kingdom, who were residing in Rome.

Romans 11:25-32;

"For I would not, brethren, that ye should be ignorant of this mystery, lest ye should be wise in your own conceits;

that blindness in part is happened to Israel, until the fulness of the Gentiles (dispersed Israelites of Northern Kingdom) be come in. And so all Israel shall be saved: as it is written, There shall come out of Sion the Deliverer (Jesus), and shall turn away ungodliness from Jacob (all Israel): For this is my covenant unto them, when I shall take away their sins.

As concerning the gospel, they are enemies for your sakes (those that refused to accept Christ): but as touching the election, they are beloved for the father's sakes.

For the gifts and calling of God are without repentance (God does not regret His doings).

For as ye in times past have not believed God, yet have now obtained mercy through their unbelief: even so have these also now not believed, that through your mercy they also may obtain mercy. (Israel obtained mercy, because the religious authorities in Judah rejected Christ, but they also obtained mercy because of Israel's former unbelief in God)

For God hath concluded them all in unbelief, that he might have mercy upon all."

Acts 5:30-31;

"The God of our fathers raised up Jesus, whom ye slew

and hanged on a tree. Him hath God exalted with his right hand to be a Prince and a Saviour, for to give repentance to Israel, and forgiveness of sins."

Isaiah 45:17;

"But Israel shall be saved in the Lord with an everlasting salvation: ye shall not be ashamed nor confounded world without end."

The end of the current dispensation will end in war. We read in,

Mathew 24:29-31;

"Immediately after the tribulation of those days shall the sun be darkened, and the moon shall not give her light, and the stars shall fall from heaven, and the powers of the heavens shall be shaken:

And then shall appear the sign of the Son of Man in heaven: and then shall all the tribes of the earth mourn, and they shall see the Son of man coming in the clouds of heaven with power and great glory.

And he shall send his angels with a great sound of a trumpet, and they shall gather together his elect from the four winds, from one end of heaven to the other."

The tribulation mentioned is, the end of Deuteronomy 28 slavery. The sun and moon darkened by flying debris and smoke resulting from the war. Stars are satellites.

His elect are the children of Israel as per,

Isaiah 45:4-5;

*"For Jacob my servant's sake, and Israel **mine elect**, I have even called thee by thy name: I have surnamed thee, though thou hast not known me. I am the Lord, and there is none else, there is no God beside me: I girded thee, though thou hast not known me:"*

Revelation 7:1-4;

"And after these things I saw four angels standing on the four corners of the earth, holding the four winds of the earth, that the wind should not blow on the earth, nor on the sea, nor on any tree. And I saw another angel ascending from the east, having the seal of the living God: and he cried with a loud voice to the four angels, to whom it was given to hurt the earth and the sea, saying, Hurt not the earth, neither the sea, nor the trees, till we have sealed the servants of our God in their foreheads.

And I heard the number of them which were sealed: and there were sealed an hundred and forty and four thousand of all the tribes of the children of Israel."

(The four angels are preventing the start of the war that will erupt. The end of the current dispensation will end in war.)

So, what do I "as Israelite" need to do to be saved?

Salvation as we have seen is the preserve of the Israelites. Jesus came to show us the way, be the sacrificial lamb of God that takes away all sins of His children; past, present and future. He did not pay this ransom so that sin can abound, but for those in Him to live righteous lives (Mathew 15:24).

Against popular belief, Gods laws were not done away with by the sacrifice of Jesus - rather the laws as a school master's guide were removed and we are justified by faith. This is why the use of sacrificial animals is no longer necessary, for the blood of Jesus cleanses all. This is not a license to sin for we are held to a higher standard. In the law, the command against adultery states "thou shalt not commit adultery." In this law we are prohibited from having carnal knowledge with unqualified partners, but in the new dispensation, even imagining and contriving in your mind is a sin. In the law about killing, it states "thou shalt not kill" they killed Jesus through the Romans thereby absolving and justifying themselves from this sin. With the new dispensation planning is as much a sin as the actual deed. If we say the law was done away with, then there would be no sin, for sin is the transgression of God's laws. For the Israelite, one needs to accept their transgression, repent, ask for forgiveness and continue living by God's laws, not as a school master but under the grace of God. But let's hear from the preacher-

Ecclesiastes 12:13-14;

"Let us hear the conclusion of the whole matter: Fear God, and keep his commandments: for this is the whole duty of man.

For God shall bring every work into judgment, with every secret thing, whether it be good, or whether it be evil."

Chapter 12

CONCLUSION

The journey through this narrative has been long, onerous, sometimes sad, mostly exiting as we delved into the interwoven intricacies of our people. The traps, innuendos and blatant lies of commission and omission were many. If it were not for the love of our people, who have been blinded, this journey would have been impossible. I believe our God is directing us to wake up from this slumber that is on us. We are to shake and shrug out of firmly held believes that we have been fed. The only sure source of information is the bible. It's our history and the guide that the Almighty God has given us. They have lied to us and made us outsiders of our heritage, but God will not be mocked. He even used our enemies to safeguard our records, culture and knowledge. He let them assume our identity to their destruction, for they lied and subjugated us using this knowledge.

As we set out to rediscover our heritage, it was obvious that we had to start with our Patriarch-Jacob. This would have made the journey shorter, but for the sake of naysayers within us, we had to retrace our steps from

Noah. This was to establish a foundation to build on. With this understanding it became clear the bible would be our main source of information. Other sources were historical records found in public domain and folk role among others. More information is still being found to authenticate what we have learned here.

We have established that the children of Israel or the Israelites are also known as Judah, Israel, Jews, the elect, children of promise, saints, sometimes Gentiles, jewels of God among others but mostly, **the children of God**. They are "the apple of His eye." The LORD walked with our fore fathers and incubated us in Egypt where we grew from 70 in number to become abundant and feared. We were thereafter persecuted, and He rescued us. After our sojourn in Egypt the LORD established a covenant with His children whereby He promised us immeasurable blessings if we stayed true to Him, but unimaginable curses if we strayed. Of course, we choose the road of rebellion to our destruction and despite many warnings we finally fell to subjugation from our enemies. By and by we were routed out of our homeland Israel aka Canaan. In 722 B.C.E. the Northern Kingdom (ten tribes) aka Israel was destroyed by the Assyrians. They were taken captive and never came back home as a nation. The Assyrian empire fell in 612 B.C.E. and the ten tribes of Israel were dispersed into the four winds. By 70 C.E. the kingdom of Judah (Judah, Benjamin and Levi) aka the Southern kingdom was defeated by the Romans with great slaughter and routed out. By 135 C.E. Israel was no more.

We have seen that whenever Israel needed refuge they would turn to their cousins through Noah in Africa. One of the reasons they did so was visage. The Israelites are Semitic and are black like the Egyptians who are Hamites and they were neighbors. They could blend in. When the kingdom of Judah fell, those that were not killed were sold as slaves, those that escaped would naturally run to Egypt. This they did, but this time they were being pursued, and they kept on going into Africa, and disappeared.

We now have the whole of Israel in diaspora. There are records and folk role stories that the Israelites started migrating from the main camp of Israel even before the exodus. Just before the war between Israel and Judah we have others migrating, not willing for brother to fight brother. We have others migrating before the Assyrian conquest. We have others migrating from Judah before the Romans besieged Jerusalem.

The dispersal of the Israelites into Africa and elsewhere was a conundrum. The Israelites dispersed and disappeared without trace. Their history went blank. Nobody could say for sure where they went. But, God always left a clue for us. He knew one day we will wake up and start looking. And like those detective stories you read when you were young, only special people could unravel the mystery or follow the clues. These would be family or colleagues with special relationships. In our case here who, but the family? When the Israelites disappeared, another type or kind of people appeared or emerged. These people were on the move, especially in Africa where they were migrating all over like something was after them, and there was. They became known as the Bantus. Now the Bantus are all over the world going by many names.

One of the most telling scenarios is the fulfillment of Deuteronomy 28:49 alluding to slavery in the Americas, and verse 68 showing that they were to retrace the Sinai route into slavery, then carried by ships and nobody would redeem them. Since the dispersion was to the four corners of the world, there is only one tribe representing Israel that this prophesy must allude to. And that is the tribe of JUDAH. According to Genesis 49:10 and other scriptures Judah would hold the rulership of Israel forever. In diaspora, wherever Judah is, that's where Israel is. The tribe of Judah after being routed out of Jerusalem-the seat of authority, they went into Africa and managed to establish the kingdom of Judah in West Africa. In West Africa they were captured by the Africans and Arabs then sold to the Europeans, who took them to American slavery in ships. This is the infamous trans-Atlantic slave trade. Please note, other Israelites were also enslaved in the Americas and elsewhere, but it is safe to say Judah ended up in America. This will shock many; the financiers, ship owners, slave auction block owners and plantation owners in the transatlantic slave trade were the current occupiers of Palestine, who call themselves Jews.

We see communities that settled in Ethiopia and beyond. We have communities that went to southern Africa through Saudi Arabia. There are distinct communities in places like Uganda in East Africa. We had the kingdom of Judah in West Africa. There are Israelites all over the world. When the Assyrian Empire fell, the Israelites could have dispersed in any direction even back home to Judah, but their affinity to Africa would have beckoned them. On close examination we know that Judah and his brethren were also referred to as Negros. This term denoting black was not used on the Africans who were also black. It's obvious the Negro was no African and the name was there to distinguish him from the African.

I know I'm Israelite, for now I do not know for sure which tribe, but most likely it's the tribe of Judah, but for now it will suffice. For the sake of the naysayers I took a DNA test on myself. This is not the feel-good type they tell you about your parental per cent age from different sub groups, like 35 % Cameroon, 0.3% Native Indian etc., to make you think you are African, but I went for the Y-DNA Haplotype test. This shows you, your paternal lineage. It is only passed on from father to son. It does not matter how many great greats you have. The deviations are minimal. My results indicated that I'm E-M2 also known as E-V38 and previously known as E1b1a. This is the same group as African Americans who are Judah. In contrast the African Y-DNA Haplotype is E-V68 also known as E1b1b. From this analysis it's easy to see that the Most High preserved the Identity of the tribe of Judah through time as a beacon for the children of Israel. In view of this I'm able to link my heritage to Israel through far away African

Americans. In the current dispensation of slavery, Judah will awaken first. The awakening and preaching the gospel of Christ to the other tribes is the prelude to the coming of the end as per Matthew 24:14; *"And this gospel of the kingdom shall be preached in all the world for a witness unto all nations; and then shall the end come."*

One question I'm bound to be asked is, if you say we are the bona-fide Israelites, then who is in Israel now? I'm glad you asked! In the near past, before 1948, the colonizing power in Palestine (named so by the Romans) was Britain. In some underhand deals, the British agreed to hand over Palestine to the current occupiers, who are Ashkenazi's and Sephardic's. The Ashkenazi originated from the caucus Mountains near Russia and Sephardi are from Spain. They are Japhetic NOT Semitic. They called themselves Jews but are not Hebrew Israelites. They are converts of Judaism. Britain and its allies confederated to keep the real Israelites out of Palestine and passed a United Nations resolution establishing Israel. The United Nations, presided over this debacle without establishing who this people were.

Why is nobody looking for the Israelites, even themselves? Answer is simple, because they are allegedly in Palestine. Nothing could be further from the truth. The whole bible is about the children of God, the Israelites. It is obvious those in Israel are fake Jews. The true Israelites are the Bantus, the Negroes, but they mostly do not know.

My work here is done. I started this journey trying to establish how we as Africans sold our fellow Africans into slavery. I appreciate and thank the young African American who challenged me, I've found out more than I imagined. I know now, and he should too, we are brethren and suffer together. I'm humbled to know who I'm in the sight of our God. I'm privileged to be awakened from this slumber that afflicts our people. I know now what is needed of me. My whole duty is to serve our God to the best of my ability, to Fear Him, and keep his commandments. I know that His son, Yeshua Ha'Maschiac died for us to fulfill the law, in fulfillment of scripture, so that, whosoever (Israelites) believeth in Him should not perish but have everlasting life (this is the salvation promised – in the Kingdom of God). To find and strive to live in conformity to these laws, is the duty of every awakened ISRAELITE. I recognize the elevated position the HOUSE of Judah holds in our awakening. I'm looking forward to it, for it is the trigger for that which is to come, OUR SALVATION. The end of Esau and the beginning of Jacob.

May all Praises, Glory and Adoration be to our father, the Most High God YAHAWAH and his son Yeshua Ha'Mashiach our salvation.

Shalom Israel!

Made in the USA
Columbia, SC
14 December 2022

73909634R00104